praise

When Despair Meets Delight

Despite the confessions of prominent politicians, sports greats, and media stars, mental illness remains a difficult subject for people to understand and discuss. This is particularly true in the church where people turn for help with their own emotional problems and sometimes find suspicion and rejection. Tony Roberts' agonizing and painful story will be a great help to many, both inside and outside the church. He offers practical ways of responding to the age-old phenomenon of mental illness so that people find healing with others and with God.

John M. Mulder,

Former President, Louisville Presbyterian Theological Seminary

Editor of *Finding God: A Treasury of Conversion Stories*

Tony Roberts understands the despair of mental illness. Because of his unique lived experience, he writes *When Despair Meets Delight* and shines a light on how the church perceives those with mental illness. With Tony's dual perspective of clergy and clinical patient, we're also given a view of how those with mental illness see the church, and thus we all are challenged to do better. Tony challenges us to stop accepting the status quo and bring the truth to the light.

Katie R. Dale

Author of *But Deliver Me from Crazy: A Memoir*

Part writing ministry, part memoir, and part meditation on the psalms, Roberts's book is well worth reading for anyone interested in spirituality, mental health, and the realm where the two co-exist. Honest and straightforward, not skating around the difficult subjects, When *Despair Meets Delight* is sure to open conversations on how serious mental illness affects ministry, and vice-versa.

Janet Coburn

Author of *Bipolar Me*

~❖~

WHEN DESPAIR MEETS DELIGHT

Stories to Cultivate Hope for Those Battling Mental Illness

a
Way With Words
publishing
Columbus, Indiana
USA

Tony Roberts

Tony Roberts / A Way With Words Publishing

2527 Franklin Street
Columbus, Indiana 47201

a
Way With Words
publishing
Columbus, Indiana
USA

www.delightindisorder.com

Publisher's Note:

*While all stories in this book are true, some names and identifying information
have been changed to protect the privacy of the individuals involved.*

When Despair Meets Delight / **Tony Roberts** -- 1st ed.

Paperback ISBN: 978-1-7350617-0-2

E-book ISBN: 978-1-0878-8900-9

Audio ISBN: 978-1-735-0617-2-6

FOREWORD

Most pastors would be shocked to know how many people in their church family live with or are directly impacted by mental illness. Stigma continues to keep mental illness silent in the church. Parents who sit in church pews week after week feel completely alone in bearing the pain of their son's or daughter's mental illness because they are embarrassed or afraid to say anything. The person sitting next to them may be carrying the same burden but who would know. And they will continue to carry these burdens alone until the church is willing to talk about it.

Tony Roberts is well positioned to help pastors and church leaders walk alongside those affected by mental illness. He writes from the perspective of a pastor, as well as one who lives with his own bipolar diagnosis.

Tony knows the ups and downs, the times of mania and depression and cycling between the two, the longing to live for Christ and the voice that sometimes tells him he would be better off dead. He writes as one who has been a patient in the psych unit of less than pleasant hospitals and one who holds a seminary degree, who has stood in the pulpit and sat by the bedside of those who are suffering.

Tony's insights for how pastors and church leaders might develop ministries for those impacted by mental illness are not merely theoretical. They are born out of real-life experience. Tony's offerings take the reader to places he has been walking side by side, sitting one on one or with groups of people who live with struggles related to their own mental health. He has coached, consulted, and advised church workers who have sought him out, as they seek to care for others who live with their own mental health challenges.

He has facilitated group training sessions for church and community leaders who want to not only reflect the heart of Jesus to those in their congregation living with some form of mental illness, but who also desire helpful tools in doing so. Tony's co-leadership of Faithful Friends, a peer led group for those who live with mental illness has stood the test of time, continuing to provide much needed support for those who attend.

I have seen Tony in action. He is real, and sometimes raw. What you see is what you get. Tony does not claim to have all the answers. His is not a pre-packaged program. He is sensitive to the local setting and those of whom it is composed.

Tony has learned to take one day at a time in his own life journey and in the calling God has set before him. Some days are better for Tony than others. Sometimes his illness rages within. The same can be true of our ministry with those who live with mental illness. Today may be two steps forward and tomorrow may be three steps backward.

Tony Roberts offers practical helps and insights for pastors and church leaders who have a genuine interest in reflecting the heart of Jesus to those who are more often than not ignored, even by the Body of Christ. If you sincerely desire to enter and remain in this journey with those who are dearly loved by God, those whose minds, for whatever reason are impacted by illness, then this is a must read. May God give you compassion, insight, wisdom, patience, and perseverance as you join Tony in this journey!

Mark Teike, *Pastor*

St. Peter's Lutheran Church, Columbus, IN

~❖~

WHEN DESPAIR
MEETS DELIGHT

STORIES FOR THOSE BATTLING MENTAL ILLNESS

Also by Tony Roberts

Delight in Disorder

When Despair Meets Delight

PROLOGUE

What's in a name?

My aim in all I say and in all I write is to speak the truth in love. This is important in all communication. It is essential in such matters of the mind and spirit.

Establishing linguistic boundaries is beyond the scope of this work, but I do want to clarify one cluster of terms with which those of us in the mental health/mental illness advocacy world wrestle.

Should I say I battle a mental health diagnosis, issue, challenge, illness, a serious mental illness, or maybe a brain disorder? How can I address a broad range of persons whose brains work in vastly different and mysterious ways? Do I speak broadly so as not to offend, or can I be specific in the hopes that many can identify.

The medical and social language of what I address here is constantly evolving. Over the course of my writing, I moved from viewing my condition as a "mental illness" to a "serious mental illness," and then a "brain illness." I have come to conclude that for now this is the most accurate and respectful way to refer to those of us whose minds betray us.

But you'll note a number of inconsistencies in this book which I opted to leave for various reasons. I maintained "mental illness" in the title because I thought that would be best understood by the most people. I called what I do "mental health ministry" because I reach out not only to those diagnosed with brain diseases like bipolar disorder, schizophrenia, and major depression, but also with others facing troubled minds. In some places I adopted my now preferred term "brain illnesses" even when I feared many people wouldn't get it.

We may find in the coming years that the way we speak about these issues is archaic as the "demon possession" of Bible times. But we do the best we can with the knowledge we now have, doing our best to get it right, to speak the truth in love. And so, in that spirit, I present this loving yet wholly fallible book.

To Veston E. Roberts, the best dad ever

Contents

INTRODUCTION

tell me the story

Tell me the same old story,

When you have cause to fear

That this world's empty glory

Is costing me too dear;

And when the Lord's bright glory

Is dawning on my soul,

Tell me the old, old story:

Christ Jesus makes thee whole.

Kathryn Hankey

Tell them what you're going to say.
Say it.
Then, tell them what you said.

Fifteen words from my first preaching class helped me shape over 500 sermons. They've also helped me become a better writer. These three sentences may not produce salvation, but they can contribute to better understanding and prompt more faithful action.

This book is about mental health ministry. It's not a "how-to" book. I can not tell you what will work in your ministry setting. Instead of answering the question, "How do we do mental health ministry?" I want to challenge you, "What difference can we make for those impacted by mental illness?"

To do this, I will tell stories of my own life and ministry. Statistics are essential, but unless they are enfleshed with stories, they won't lead to change. Evidence-based programs may produce proposals for getting grants, but if faith communities are going to carry out our God-given mission, we need to get to know persons with mental illness and invite and involve them in kingdom work.

What credentials do I have to write such a book? There are those in a standard bio: a Master of Divinity degree with Christian counseling concentration; eight credits in Clinical Pastoral Education; 18 years of pastoral ministry; and over a decade as a faith & mental health advocate.

All these qualify me as an expert on the subject, but nothing has prepared me to write this book more than living an examined 56 years with bipolar disorder.

I have three goals in all I write:

- Foster spiritual friendships with those living with a mental illness

- Encourage loved ones caring for those battling brain illnesses

- Equip faith leaders to better respond to persons with troubled minds.

When people asked Jesus what they must do to be saved, he told stories.

The kingdom of God is like... a banquet for beggars... a woman finding... a lost coin... an outsider lifting a wounded man out of the ditch and providing for his care.

Rabbi Jesus, how shall we do mental health ministry?

Ah, let me tell you a story.

DIAGNOSING THE PROBLEM

If I can't feel, if I can't move, if I can't think, and I can't care, then what conceivable point is there in living?

Kay Redfield Jamison

But now, LORD, what do I look for?
My hope is in you.

Psalm 39.7

CHAPTER ONE

prognosis

Rev. Roberts, you have bipolar disorder.

What? I was in a medication-induced stupor. My mind was in a haze. Was I dreaming? Bipolar? I'd heard of it, but couldn't connect with it. What did it mean for me? I couldn't take it in, so I turned over and went back to sleep. Maybe dreams would take this dreadful diagnosis away or at least infuse the hope I needed to handle this new reality.

Rest wouldn't come as I tossed in a hypervigilant wakefulness, staring beyond the walls. I got up and walked to the central nurse's station. The nurse on duty wore a gentle and kind expression. She had a glow about her and seemed to float above her rotating chair.

She asked what I was looking for. I told her the diagnosis I was given, the one I wished to understand. Suddenly, her expression turned dour and her glow became a dark cloud. She spoke with otherworldly authority I felt too frail to question.

"You will get a divorce. You will no longer work in pastoral ministry. You will spend the rest of your life in and out of psych hospitals."

Was she for real? I don't know. It may have been a nightmare. Indeed, it was a nightmare, but it also happened. This was February of 1995. I was 31 years old. I was married, had two young children ages two, and not quite a year and I was pastor of a village church poised to grow. I was publishing articles, devotions, and reviews in an increasing number of journals and magazines. Now I was faced with the prospect of it all coming to a screeching halt.

I lay in bed lost in a cognitive fog, weary but restless. I was weighed down by a foreboding sense of a bleak future. Paralyzed by grief, I cried; loud sobs. Wails, and moans flowed from a void in my soul I had not known before.

No one heard. No one came. No one comforted me. While I believed God was with me in this dark valley, it seemed God was mocking me, putting me in my place for sins unknown. The notion God was hemming me in offered no assurance. In that moment, I felt God was not a loving Father but a malicious dictator, emasculating me on a divine whim.

In the midst of spiritual paralysis, I found strength to get up. I opened the door and walked down the hall, not knowing where I was going or what I would find. Then, a young man with gentle features appeared by my side. He laid his hand on my shoulder and led me to a cushioned couch in the lounge.

I poured out my soul to him. Longing for my former life and anger at what life was now with fear of what it would become. I told him the prognosis I had been given: Divorce. Unemployment. Hospitalization. How could I possibly handle this? He looked at me with a soft yet penetrating gaze and said, *It doesn't have to be that way.*

I breathed in these encouraging words. Was he an angel sent by God or just an aide working third-shift? Were his words prophetic or just wishful assurance? Time would tell. In that moment, however, they were just enough to suggest a glimmer of hope on the horizon.

I never saw that angelic aide again. But I remember his words well and find comfort in them on nights I fear a bleak future. I share this reassurance when I sit with someone on a psych unit, in my support group circle, or over coffee with someone cast under a shadow of despair.

It doesn't have to be that way.

*I look back over my shoulder and feel the presence of an intense young
girl and then a volatile and disturbed young woman, both with high
dreams and restless, romantic aspirations.*

Kay Redfield Jamison

*Where can I go from your Spirit?
Where can I flee from your presence?
If I go up to the heavens, you are there;
if I make my bed in the depths, you are there.*

Psalm 139.7-8

CHAPTER TWO

first episode

Being a basketball prodigy weaving wonders on a small-town court in Southern Indiana during the heyday of Hoosier Hysteria is as close to being a god as many ever will be. People ask when symptoms of my bipolar disorder began to surface, and it is hard to separate the exaggerated praise I received from the delusions of grandeur I conceived.

Was my clear conviction that a film crew was recording every movement I made for a future feature documentary a grandiose hallucination or just a young boy's healthy fantasy? Was vomiting after every loss a sign of a chemical disorder or overcompetitiveness?

Had I not developed more problematic symptoms later in life, I doubt I would make much of these instances. Even as it is, I choose to consider my pre-teen years as extraordinary only in their ordinariness. I was in good relational shape; my family stood beside me. I was in intellectual shape; an honor student in a reputable school. I was in physical shape; a top athlete in both tennis and basketball. I was even in spiritual shape, practicing my personal faith with prayer, Bible study, worship, and fellowship within a supportive faith community.

Then came the day in my sophomore Algebra II class, when Mr. Lang handed out a routine test. I was eager to see if I could advance my average to move from second to first on the list of best ever students in his class. That was when it happened.

A voice, not my own, came from the ceiling, the surrounding walls, the hallway, and through the window. It was deep, commanding me to fail. Deafening, I set the test aside and looked around. Nothing. Still, the voice. I asked for a hall pass. I went to the restroom, rubbed water on my face and looked in the mirror. This must be in my head. But it was so real.

I returned to my seat and finished the exam. Eventually, the voice subsided. For awhile. But it would come back -- again, and again, until it became my constant companion.

According to the National Alliance on Mental Illness (NAMI), the average age of onset for bipolar disorder is 25, but symptoms can occur in the teens. Navigating bipolar can be difficult. Often one with bipolar becomes lost, crippled by mood states that demand attention and distract him/her from pursuing a vocational path or entering into a healthy relationship. From a financial perspective, it is next to impossible to hold down a job and establish healthcare benefits.

I was fortunate that while my symptoms began in my teen years, they did not become debilitating until my thirties. I've often wondered what contributed to my good fortune. I believe it was the grace of God, grace working through a loving family, a solid faith foundation, and encouraging coaches and teachers who kept me focused on doing my best.

Not all young people with bipolar have such a safety net. For many, the best way they know to escape the ravages of mental illness is through drug use, often called, *self-medicating*. Getting stoned or drunk gives us false perception we are effectively managing our moods. They take the edge off our madness, if only for a while. They can even quiet the voices and give us a measure of peace. When my safety net began to fray, I would find this out firsthand.

~❖~

I have the choice of being constantly active and happy or introspectively passive and sad. Or I can go mad by ricocheting in between.

Sylvia Plath

In the LORD I take refuge.
How then can you say to me:
Flee like a bird to your mountain.

Psalm 11.1

~❖~

CHAPTER THREE

self medicating

Someone has told you that you are a good actor. They were wrong.

Doc Evans spoke with all the compassionate honesty he could muster. I got a C- in Acting. It hurt like hell, but at least it gave me a better sense of my vocation. I knew not to pursue a career on Broadway.

But Doc Evans didn't just crush a young man's dream. He had read some of my work in the campus newspaper. Write me a play, he said. Doc had inspired the careers of several who wrote for the stage, screen, and television. Just a few years earlier, one of Doc's students, Jim Leonard, penned the award-winning play The Diviners. Doc's invitation for me to explore creative writing were not empty words. They meant a great deal to me. I've yet to write the play Doc requested. But I have spent over 35 years now honing my craft of weaving words, shaping sentences, and parsing out paragraphs to make sense of what can seem like a senseless world.

Hanover College in the early 1980s was a good place for me to explore who I was and what I would do. It was a time of letting go and launching out. I gave up tennis and basketball. Instead, I jumped into classic literature and philosophy with reckless abandon. I picked the brains of my professors as I scanned the book titles on their shelves. I discussed what it means to be human with a group of Hub-Rats, (named after the campus coffee shop). I gave up Izod labels for Salvation Army attire, like a bowling shirt with a "Harold" name patch emblazoned on the left chest.

What was I thinking? Where was my mind in all this? Like Plath and many others with bipolar disorder, I was cycling from the depths of despair to the heights of elation, often mixed together in a single moment. I would bemoan the misery of existence while cackling over the absurdity of human affairs. My saving grace is that I did not take myself too seriously. My damaging instinct is that I could not find it within myself to take much of anything seriously. It hurt too much.

Some dismiss the emotional pain of college students as nothing more than angst, nagging worry about trivial matters. But for those experiencing it, angst is anything but trivial. It is a deep dread about the human condition, or the state of world affairs. For those vulnerable to mental health disorders, such dread can lead to a state of psychological paralysis. For those of us with mental illness, angst is often the trigger that sets off a chemical explosion which manifests itself in destructive emotions and damaging behaviors.

So what was I to do? It was the early 1980s. No one was talking about mental illness. Depression and anxiety were not viewed as clinical disorders, and there was not a single counselor on staff at my college. Persons with bipolar disorder or schizophrenia had few options. Medication was imprecise. Therapies were unproven. Through my college years, I was taught that my extreme emotional states were caused by a toxic cultural environment, beginning with my family. The best thing I could do to maintain my sanity was blame my mother. And, as the child of a divorce, the best way to blame my mother was to be just like my father.

~❖~

Someone once said that every man is trying to live up to his father's expectations or make up for their father's mistakes

Barack Obama

What mean ye, that ye use this proverb concerning the land of Israel, saying, The fathers have eaten sour grapes, and the children's teeth are set on edge?

Ezekiel 18.2, KJV

CHAPTER FOUR

family history

Growing up, my dad was my hero. Dad describes himself as *just a dumb old Kentuckian with a sixth-grade education*. He can be sharp as a tack, but this self-deprecation keeps him from abandoning his hillbilly ancestors. To this day, he remains, *just as common as an old shoe*.

Back in the day, Dad was a drinker who would consume many *cans of courage* on *liquid lunches*, to cope with a job he despised, and war wounds battling abject poverty, inherited shame, and family betrayal. Much stemmed from his father, Joe Etsy. Dad vowed early in boyhood to never be like his father, and, from what I can tell, he never has.

One time when my Dad was visiting, I was in a "mixed state." This is when bleak frustration of depression joins the irritable rage of mania. I lashed out verbally at my wife in the presence of my father, something I would never do in my right mind. I pounded my fist on the counter, then paced around in a tight circle. Dad stood still in the corner, clearly distressed.

As quickly as I raged, I relaxed. I apologized to my wife, then to Dad. He forgave me, but he said something I'll never forget. *That's just like your Grandpa used to get.*

Grandpa Joe Etsy's life and death weigh heavily on the conscience of our family. I never knew him, as he died before I was born. My Grandma Roberts never spoke of him to me. I've only pieced his story together from torn memories his children -- my aunts and uncles -- have entrusted to me. Stitched together, the memories portray a man with a restless spirit and a troubled mind who never settled down to become the father his eight children desperately needed.

If you talk to Dad's oldest brother, Jack, he'll share fond memories of his father. He remembers numerous visits to spend time with relatives, working together on a small family farm in Martinsville, going to the Bean Blossom Bluegrass Festival where they saw Bill Monroe and Mother Maybelle Carter. Clearly, Joe Etsy did some things right even though he saddled with poverty, a lack of education, and became a father to so many at such an early age.

But, as Dad recounts it, something happened to Joe Etsy around the time Jack left for the military. He became volatile. His body would become stiff. He would fall to the ground. He began to sleep in the coal shed and left behind any sense of personal hygiene.

Joe Etsy never went to the doctor. He couldn't afford one. Even if he could, his pride wouldn't let him. What would a doctor have done, anyway? Diagnostic skills and treatment options for what he was experiencing were decades away.

One night, in the middle of a blizzard, Joe Etsy decides he is going to walk to the store for cigarettes. Grandma pleads with him not to go. They argue. It becomes fierce. Finally, he tells her to go to bed, that he is just going out to the coal shed to get something.

Time passes. The blizzard lets up. Grandma sends their youngest boy, my Uncle Larry, out to the coal shed, to check on his father. As soon as Larry steps out of the door, he sees emergency lights in the distance, shining on a figure below. A figure big enough to be a man is lying still in the middle of the road.

Truth about tragedy can be hidden for lifetimes. Mysteries may never be solved. Over the years, I've developed quite a few notions about stories handed down to me of Joe Etsy's death.

On the surface, it could be that Joe Etsy was just bound and determined to get those cigarettes. The drifting snow kept him from walking along the side of the road and blinded the driver such that he couldn't steer away.

I've also thought perhaps he started walking and had a seizure, throwing his body into the road and leaving him incapacitated to get up when the truck came along.

But then I think of Dad's words to me when I had an episode. *I know what it is like to lose control. I know what it is like to be filled with rage and have nothing to do with it. I know how much self-loathing can eat you up inside.*

Maybe Joe Etsy looked out at that blinding snow and, somewhere in the middle of the road, saw a way to escape.

I have absolutely no pleasure in the stimulants in which I sometimes so madly indulge. It has not been in the pursuit of pleasure that I have periled life and reputation and reason. It has been the desperate attempt to escape from torturing memories, from a sense of insupportable loneliness and a dread of some strange impending doom.

Edgar Allan Poe

Share with the LORD's people who are in need.
Practice hospitality.

Romans 12.13

CHAPTER FIVE

spiritual encounter

I had a good friend in college, Steve Franz, who used to say, *I drink and smoke because they are the best ways I know to commit suicide in a manner deemed acceptable by society.* I'm convinced no one really wants to kill themselves. We just want to stop the pain. We want to silence the voices.

According to the National Survey on Drug Use and Health, 9.2 million U.S. adults experienced both mental illness and a substance use disorder in 2018.. Among those addicted to drugs or alcohol, as many as half have a clinical mental health diagnosis. Substances may hide symptoms for a while, they may keep the demons away for a time, but they are sure to return with a vengeance.

My own path led through a period of substance abuse. In college, it seemed a rite of passage to get drunk and stoned. Even on a daily basis. I was still able to keep my grades up, write for the campus newspaper, even serve as student body president. The waves I rode between being a despairing drunk and an enlightened pothead were my way of managing moods.

After college I was out of control. No drink was strong enough to numb my pain. No drug potent enough to pick me up out of the pit. I lived alone, spending days and nights documenting my dreadful times on an upright Smith-Corona, circa 1952.

I worked at a plastics factory, boxing up loads of bags to be sent to clothing stores. The rhythmic pounding of the machines penetrated my skull, and I started hearing the voices again, in earnest. I tried to shut them out with music, but nothing would tune out these insidious, intrusive, invasive voices.

Then, I began to hear a symphony of silence. It didn't come at once. It didn't produce a complete quietude. But it did bring a measure of harmony to the dissonance in my mind. It was a still, small voice. It soothed my searing soul.

I started attending a small country church, Grammar Presbyterian. The people there didn't mind me coming to worship smelling like burnt plastic. I don't think they knew just what to make of me, but they accepted me all the same. One of the saints, Annie Jaquess, visited my home and invited me to become a member the next Sunday.

Easter Sunday, 1983, as I was driving to church to become one of the faithful flock, I saw out of the corner of my eye an old woman pacing in a bank parking lot. I pulled over and walked up beside her. She was confused. I told her it was Sunday, the bank was closed. She spoke, but made no sense. I offered to take her home, but she couldn't tell me where she lived.

I didn't know what to do, so I invited her into my truck and took her to a neighboring church not familiar to me. We followed the crowd of well-clad worshippers along the path leading to the sanctuary. We were welcomed at the door by a man with a saintly expression shining through a weary brow.

I told him what I knew of the woman's story, that she was lost and I was trying to help her find her way home. He listened. Carefully. Prayerfully. Then he gently placed his hand on her shoulder and guided her back to a quiet room where he handed her a muffin and a cup of coffee. The warmth of his hospitality thawed the cold confusion that clouded her mind. She came to her senses. Then, after they celebrated together the new life of the Risen Christ, he took her home.

I left the church in tears, feeling embraced by the grace of God reaching out through the hands of God's saints. It wasn't just the woman who was lost.

For years, I have told this story as the pivotal event in my conversion to Christian service. I have since gone back to the church to thank them. They politely received my thanks. Yet, there is no living memory of anything of the sort happening on that Easter Sunday.

Maybe it wasn't significant enough for them to mark it as a moment to remember. Maybe the colorful banners or the record attendance or the sound of the bell choir have erased other memories of things that happened that day. I've even wondered if I dreamed it or if it was part of an elaborate hallucination. Stranger things have happened to me.

All I can say is it was a wondrous sign of how ministry can be when we are ready and willing to help people find their way home.

The next day I began the process to enroll in seminary.

DISCOVERING POSSIBILITIES

Our humanity comes to its fullest bloom in giving. We become beautiful people when we give whatever we can give: a smile, a handshake, a kiss, an embrace, a word of love, a present, a part of our life . . . all of our life.

Henri J.M. Nouwen

The people walking in darkness have seen a great light; on those living in the land of deep darkness a light has dawned.

Isaiah 9.2

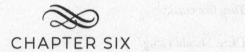

CHAPTER SIX

voiceless prayer

Louisville Presbyterian Theological Seminary (LPTS) was the obvious choice for me. It was not an elite academic institution, like Princeton, but they were equipping men and women for all realms of ministry, not just as church pastors. They were particularly known for their field education program, where students would serve in ministry while taking classes, rather than take a year off for an internship. It required the sort of balance that would be demanded of us in our vocations.

My first Field Ed assignment was at what was then called an "Institution for Persons with Severe and Profound Mental Retardation." My responsibilities included providing pastoral care for residents and staff during the week, and leading five services of worship on Sundays. I would engage in ministry for the week, then meet with my supervisor for reflection. The supervisory meetings were like intense psychotherapy as we examined not just what I did and what I could do better, but how it impacted me.

None of the residents were verbal. Some drooled incessantly. Most rocked repeatedly, strapped down in their wheelchairs. A few wore protective wrestling helmets to keep from cracking their skulls against the walls. Loud moaning was heard through the hallway and there was a constant stench of feces and urine. I was expected to be their pastor.

The first worship service I stood up front and waited for something to happen. Some inspiration or divine guidance. Instead, only rocking, drooling, moaning.

A kind aide noticed my discomfort and said,

They like music.

Okay. Should I sing?

Well, she said, *I have a tape.*

Good.

She pulled out a cassette player and put on some Bible songs. The rocking began to synchronize. The moaning, harmonize. The drooling continued, but it was somehow different. Not holy water, but not as gross either.

After about 15 minutes of song, I called for prayer. I started to speak and then it dawned on me -- they may not understand a word I say. Chances are their vocabulary would be limited to their name and maybe a few concrete terms.

I asked the aide to help me with the prayer. We went to each resident and laid our hands on their heads. She would say their names and I would follow with a brief prayer I thought they might receive as a blessing.

I went into that first worship believing I had nothing to offer. The voices in my head were screaming at me that I was an imposter. I had no idea what I was doing there. I was in a dark tunnel. Then a light shined, and I discovered I was just where I needed to be, just where I belonged.

~❖~

Things change as they are discovered.

Joel Latner

*Love the LORD your God with all your heart
and with all your soul and with all your strength
and with all your mind;
and, love your neighbor as yourself.*

Luke 10.27

CHAPTER SEVEN

group therapy

Though not as engaging as field work, my classroom experience at LPTS expanded my mind about how to become a good minister. Of all the academic disciplines, counseling intrigued me most. It was there that I discovered the depths of my own brokenness and began to believe that, in spite of this brokenness, I could be a wounded healer.

David Steere was not only Chair of the Counseling department, he was the department. A few others came along in my later years, but my mind had been transformed by Dr. Steere, and it became hard-set. For years I tried to mimic his intense gaze and dynamic voice when I'd counsel others, but I gave up when I discovered he was only human. And so I am.

While housed in a seminary, the counseling I learned was not Christian in any conventional sense of the term. We learned from the theorists and therapists who moved beyond individual psychoanalysis to "family systems." We studied pioneers like Virginia Satir and Milton Erickson, who did not espouse a shared doctrine, but together they believed a person could be more "self-actualized" if the family was brought together and relational equilibrium was established.

I was fascinated with this approach to human understanding. It also made me miserable. I felt so out of touch with my own family, and the interactions I had left me full of despair and anger.

At Dr. Steere's suggestion, I entered group therapy. Each week I would gather in a circle with people who also felt maladjusted. Bruce, the therapist, kept the conversation flowing. Any given week we would discuss issues like self-esteem, hair pulling, parenting, anxiety, work troubles. I was affirmed, but it didn't go anywhere. I would leave on Tuesday afternoon feeling better, but by Tuesday night, I was an emotional mess.

Little did I know that while I was talking about such things as asking a girl out on a date, chemicals in my brain were sending signals to my soul that I was nobody, that I had no purpose, and that my life was not worth living.

This was 1987. In December of that year, Prozac, *the happy pill*, was approved by the Food and Drug Administration. In 1989. Prozac became the first, among many, psychotropics I would take.

In my years of mental health treatment, I've found the recovery process requires a holistic approach. Prayer and pills. Worship and therapy. Fellowship and support groups. If our body, mind, and spirit are left disconnected, they remain diseased. Only when we allow God to fill our whole selves with divine love can we be healed.

~❖~

*If at first you don't succeed, destroy all evidence
that you tried.*

Steven Wright

*Let perseverance finish its work so that you may be mature and com-
plete, not lacking anything.*

James 1.4

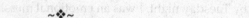

CHAPTER EIGHT

anointing moment

Hey Russell, this is Carter. I got a guy here who needs another year. His name is Tony Roberts.

My journey through seminary was full of detours and dead-ends. I had some close friends. I made good grades. I had fun co-authoring satirical newsletters. But I could be curt with my classmates. I didn't study much and once got a zero on an exam. While taking on false idols with irony, I also hurt people in genuine pain.

In my senior year of seminary, I was terrified to start my career before finding a wife. So I desperately clung to a toxic relationship all the while sabotaging my pastoral pursuit with failed efforts in field education, the classroom, and ordination exams. God was tugging at me to move forward, and I was pulling back with all the weight in my own body and all the hangers-on I could grab.

That's when another angel entered my life. George Carter was my field education director. He also had worked extensively as a pastoral counselor. I went to him first for a conflictual relationship I had with a supervisor. He tried to mediate and when that didn't work, he made his office available for hour-long cry sessions.

Dr. Carter also taught Polity, sort of the rules and regulations of running a church. Mostly, it was rote memorization, not rocket science. How hard is it to remember to open and close church meetings in prayer and write it down in the minutes? Something about Polity froze my brain. What became clear to Dr. Carter and eventually to me is I was not psychologically ready to enter a church meeting where I would be expected to lead. I was barely ready to enter a church at all.

With only weeks remaining in my senior year, I had no plan of what I'd do next. I walked into Dr. Carter's office and pleaded my case. There were tears involved. Many. He calmly listened then did one of the most compassionate things a person has ever done for me. He picked up the phone and dialed a friend of his about giving me a chaplain internship.

The image I have of Dr. Carter holding that phone to his ear is embedded in my mind. It was the first of what would be many anointing moments: Walking across the stage as I graduated from seminary. Elders laying on hands and praying over me. Hearing for the first time my daughter's helpless yet hopeful cry. Then again with another daughter. Breathing in the courtroom austerity where I would be confirmed fit to father three. Then four.

These senses cradle me in meaning when my mind has become senseless, giving purpose, pointing the way forward when I become lost. Like the woman lost in the bank parking lot, the experience of being heard helps me find my way home.

~❖~

The function of prayer is not to influence God, but rather to change the nature of the one who prays.

Soren Kierkegaard

In the morning, LORD, you hear my voice;
in the morning I lay my requests before you
and wait expectantly.

Psalm 5.3

~❖~

cracked pot

CHAPTER NINE

cracked pot

St. Luke's Episcopal-Presbyterian Hospital is nestled in a quaint western suburb of St. Louis known as Chesterfield. Their motto, "Our Specialty is You," is played out in the personal care patients receive by multi-disciplinary staff. As much of a cliche as this is, I found St. Luke's to offer healing for me as a student chaplain, and, through my service there, for patients, families, and staff.

My ministry flowed from the Pastoral Care department. Under the supervision of Ed Healthcock and Bill Russell and working alongside half a dozen other interns, I did my best to contribute to St. Luke's healing mission -- leading worship, serving communion, praying at bedsides. Once, I even baptized a dead infant, putting pastoral care before denominational polity.

While we were paid interns, the primary focus was on our education. Clinical Pastoral Education (CPE) is considered by many pursuing ministry a grueling process. In it, our psyches were held under microscopes. The wings of our vocation were clipped to examine the dirt inside the feathers. We engaged in, reflected on, composed, then presented ministry episodes as case studies to be reviewed by both supervisors and peers. If you showed a notable flaw, it could be scrutinized for an hour. If the report seemed too perfect, you might be accused of being inauthentic, hiding something. CPE was a make or break proposition for many. If you survived, you were strengthened for church combat. If not, well, you were likely saved from spiritual suicide.

I had a mostly miserable time at St. Luke's. I now see that my heart was not in it. I did not give enough of myself to the ministry there to grow. And when this was pointed out, I became defensive and withdrew. I held great respect.for both Rev. Heathcock and Rev. Russell but resented them at the same time. Looking back, I see them as father figures who spoke the truth in love and modeled the best of what I would become as a minister.

My saving grace during this period was the first thirty minutes of each day, when morning prayers were said in the chapel. I came to cherish the rhythm and routine of reading regularly through Scripture, and speaking words that have been shaped by the spiritual lives of saints throughout the ages. Here in the chapel each morning, I took in enough fresh air to make it through days I was only holding my breath.

Over the course of that year, in spite of my best efforts to resist it, prayer changed me. I started to relax. I went for after-lunch walks. I told jokes. I revealed my vulnerabilities and examined my flaws. I became, as Rev. Russell would call me at my ordination service, a "Cracked Pot."

When writing of oneself one should show no mercy. Yet why at the first attempt to discover one's own truth does all inner strength seem to melt away in floods of self-pity and tenderness and rising tears . . .

Georges Bernanos

This is the word that came to Jeremiah from the LORD: *"Go down to the potter's house, and there I will give you my message." So I went down to the potter's house, and I saw him working at the wheel. But the pot he was shaping from the clay was marred in his hands; so the potter formed it into another pot, shaping it as seemed best to him. Then the word of the* LORD *came to me. He said,*
"Can I not do with you, Israel, as this potter does?"
declares the LORD. *"Like clay in the hand of the potter,*
so are you in my hand, Israel.

Jeremiah 18.1-6

CHAPTER TEN

pastoral support

I became a husband, a pastor, and a father in the span of about a year. Doubts I had about how woefully unprepared I was for each role were confirmed in the weeks that followed the birth of my first child.

I had prepared a month's worth of sermons and lined up pastoral care so I could be home with my child and her mother. That first week, I focused completely on my daughter's needs: changing diapers, giving baths, reading to her. I even made a video with me singing along to Sandi Patty's (*You Are A*) *Masterpiece*.

The second week I was finished. I told my wife to bring in her mother, and I started working around the clock. Why? My underlying fear was that I would not be a good enough provider. So, in addition to doing my pastoral duties, I started writing for journals and devotional magazines. I composed a prayer booklet for the congregation I thought might result in some extra income. It didn't.

I was pursuing a creative urge only writing could satisfy by allowing the writing to consume my life. It got in the way of being a good husband, pastor, and father. When I came down from my creative highs, I sank into dark valleys, full of self-pity and remorse.

I needed help, so I saw a psychiatrist. I told her about my depression but not my highs. Who would view elation as a problem? She prescribed Prozac which didn't work. Then Wellbutrin. No go. Then Paxil. We went through nearly every second-generation antidepressant over the course of the next two years. Nothing could keep the darkness at bay. Nothing lifted me out of the pit.

Despite this, I was compensating fairly well. In college and grad school I had adapted to mood swings by working ahead when I felt good so I wouldn't fall behind when I collapsed. This became all the more important now that I was in a paid career. But the demands of providing consistent pastoral care at times overwhelmed me. I couldn't schedule funerals to fit my emotional state. Crisis intervention happened around the clock, even when I could barely drag myself from bed.

A pastor from a neighboring town saw I was struggling and took me under his wing. Ken Dobson was a former missionary who had unique skills as a preacher and teacher. He was also a powerful prayer warrior and would become a good friend. Ken picked me up every Tuesday morning and took me to a pastors' prayer gathering. Unlike other groups of pastors who sat around comparing the size of their congregations, the strength of their programs, or the amount of their stewardship campaign, this was a place where wounded warriors confessed sin and pleaded for mercy. We admitted our fears and cried over our pain; then we would lift up these raw emotions to the One who hears and heals.

While my brain continued to betray me, spiritual support gave me the stamina to make it through each week. Had it not been for this group, I would have fallen off a psychological cliff and maybe never recovered. I would have lost not only my ministry, but my mind, suffering a nervous breakdown or a psychotic episode. Maybe even a catatonic depression. God, working through these faithful friends, carried me through these days and strengthened me for what lie ahead.

~❖~

*The road to creativity passes so close to the madhouse
and often detours or ends there.*

Ernest Becker

*Look, he is coming with the clouds, and every eye will see him, even
those who pierced him; and all peoples on earth will mourn because of
him. So shall it be! Amen.*

Revelation 1.7

CHAPTER ELEVEN

february 12, 1995

How does one go from being a slightly depressed yet ambitious young pastor rising in the church ranks to being a psych patient battling bipolar disorder with psychotic features, strapped to a bed in seclusion?

Here's how I did it:

- Quit taking medication prescribed by a psychiatrist.

- Go to a retiring family doctor whose only knowledge of psychotropics came from drug representatives.

- Stay up six days and nights scheming ways to turn a sluggish congregation into a mighty army to usher in God's kingdom.

- Begin an in-depth study of the book of Revelation and modern parallels.

- Read the local news, one hand on the paper, one on the Bible, and me bleeding between.

This was my schedule the day before I got my diagnosis:

3 am Walk to church, notice our directional sign is bent to the ground. Lay hands on it and call on the blood of Jesus to conquer the forces of darkness.

4 am Pray through the newspaper.

5 am Touch up sermon on healing, with these words:

Our ailments may be blessings in disguise. As we listen to our bodies and minds and seek out care, we gain insight on how to lead more abundant lives.

6 am Review Revelation 1 for Bible study, underlining verse 7:
Look, he is coming with the clouds, and every eye will see him, even those who pierced him; and all peoples on earth will mourn because of him. So shall it be! Amen.

7 am Meet with youth leader. She is wearing sunglasses. I suspect demon possession and tell her I will lead that night instead.

8 am Prayer; sketch notes for afternoon prison service

9 am Lead Adult Sunday school on topic of Faith Healing

10 am Lead worship. During illustration of a dying child, I laugh uncontrollably.

11 am Travel thru snow to prison; Listen to R.E.M.'s *It's the End of the World as We Know It (. . . and I Feel Fine)*

1 pm Lead worship for group of women prisoners.

Begin with Isaiah 42.6-7 --I, the Lord, have called you in righteousness. I will take hold of your hand. I will keep you and make you To be a covenant for the Gentiles, To open eyes that are blind, To free captives from prison; And to release from the dungeon; Those who sit in darkness.
As I begin the message, a guard ushers me out.

2pm Embankment Crash: As snow worsens, I lose traction, do a 360 and crash into an embankment. I see a man in the distance plowing his driveway. I walk over and ask if he could help me push my car. He does. Out of gratitude, I offer to bless his house. He declines.

4pm Share communion at a nursing home. Sheer grace.

6pm Prepare for Youth Group while listening to R.E.M.'s *It's the End of the World.*

7pm Youth Service. I laugh uproariously when a light fixture falls to the ground. Youth arrive and I begin the program by playing at top volume *The End of the World.* I dance and bang my head against the walls.

That was Sunday, February 12, 1995.

The day that could well have been my last in ministry.

But God had other plans.

God moves in a mysterious way; His wonders to perform;
He plants His footsteps in the sea; And rides upon the storm. Deep in
unfathomable mines; Of never failing skill;
He treasures up His bright designs;
And works His sovereign will.
Ye fearful saints, fresh courage take;
The clouds ye so much dread. Are big with mercy and shall break; In
blessings on your head.

William Cowper

Therefore, in order to keep me from becoming conceited, I was given a
thorn in my flesh, a messenger of Satan, to torment me. Three times I
pleaded with the Lord to take it away from me. But he said to me, "My
grace is sufficient for you, for my power is made perfect in weakness."
Therefore I will boast all the more gladly about my weaknesses, so that
Christ's power may rest on me. That is why, for Christ's sake, I delight
in weaknesses, in insults, in hardships, in persecutions, in difficulties.
For when I am weak, then I am strong.

2 Corinthians 12.7b-10

~❖~

CHAPTER TWELVE

managing madness

I stayed awake through the night. It had been a week since I slept. I would go to bed for a while, but my mind raced. I tried to unravel the mysteries of God and the meaning of the universe and had thought I was close to some solutions. That night, however, I was simply scared. I knew my life was out of control, that I needed help.

The next day I admitted myself into the psych unit of Clarion hospital. There I had an episode of manic psychosis. I was certain the world was ending and that my mission was to rescue the chosen from destruction. I fueled myself with a handful of sugar cookies, then ran down the hall and into the glass security door. Then I blacked out, so all I know of the next 36 hours is what others told me.

It wasn't until Wednesday evening that the heavy fog began to lift. Somehow, I came to my senses well enough to know I had a huge decision to make. What would I tell my church? I didn't want someone else making this decision for me. I had to come up with something quick. Though the future was unclear, I certainly wouldn't be in the pulpit Sunday nor the next Session meeting. What about pastoral care? Stewardship? I was a solo pastor. There was no other paid staff in place to pick up the slack.

Through the cloudy haze of my brain, the Spirit gave me enough clarity to weigh my options. It was 1995. For most, having a mental illness meant being excluded from society as a danger to yourself and others. You were locked away in an institution, a shame to your family and friends. Many Christians believed it to be demon possession. How would church leaders respond if I revealed I had a chronic mental illness that would need treatment the rest of my life, that it could tear my family apart, and make it difficult if not impossible to return to ministry?

I don't remember just how I came to the decision, but I do know I had much wise counsel -- from church leaders, trusted colleagues, and ministry supervisors. I composed a letter which reflected on my situation with the words of Psalms. A member of the church who was a psychologist wrote an article explaining my diagnosis. Our most trusted prayer warrior crafted words calling on the Holy Spirit to guide us through the difficult days ahead. With these and a statement by the Board supporting me, they printed a special edition newsletter which they gave out the first Sunday I was gone and mailed to arrive the next day.

The church responded with tremendous compassion. The Board offered paid leave, with an assurance that I could return to ministry when I was ready. Someone paid off our extraordinary medical expenses. People offered childcare. Meals were provided. Cards, letters, fruit, and balloons filled the psych center such that the other residents thought I was some kind of rock star.

It took six months before I started preaching again. It took a year to resume my other duties. I had worried that such extended grace would wear thin, but it never did. When I returned to ministry, I was eager to do all I could to express gratitude through service. Yet, many were watching out for me to see that I didn't overdo it.

I continued to take medication. There were many side effects, such as lethargy, confusion, and extreme weight gain. But I believed my psychiatrist when he said the alternative would be much worse. I went to therapy weekly. My wife and I started seeing a couple's counselor. I sought out a spiritual guide and became part of a community prayer group. Each week, I devoted a day for family and a day for prayer and study. My life became more balanced. The boundary lines were falling in pleasant places.

Not only did my mental health improve, but our ministry expanded. I became known in the community as the pastor with a mental illness. A wounded healer. People who struggled emotionally came to me for counsel, showed up for Bible studies, and attended worship among people they had thought would shun them.

But there was also a fall-out. Several members dropped out. Some went to other churches. Gossip ensued. People started treating me with kid gloves, as if I were so fragile I would break, or so volatile I would break them. Many in the community believed I was too misguided to be a spiritual leader. In response, the elders and I made a commitment to visit every member in their homes. We would listen prayerfully and only respond as the Spirit led -- gently speaking the truth in love.

One day I knocked at the door of an elderly widow who hadn't been to church for decades. She came to the door in a housecoat and slippers, a Scottish terrier yapping at her heels.

Hello Wilma. I'm Pastor Tony.

She looked crossly into my eyes.

Are you that pastor who has a mental illness?

I bowed my head. *I am.*

Her pitch raised. *I thought mental illness is a sin?*

I spoke softly. *No, Wilma, I don't believe it is.*

Her frozen face began to thaw and she said:

I've been depressed all my life and was told I was a sinner.

Now come on in.

~❖~

*The ragamuffin who sees his life as a voyage of discovery and runs the
risk of failure has a better feel for faithfulness than the timid man who
hides behind the law and never finds out who he is at all.*

Brennan Manning

*But God chose the foolish things
of the world to shame the wise;
God chose the weak things of the world
to shame the strong.*

1 Corinthians 1.7

CHAPTER THIRTEEN

returning to ministry

Not only were things going well at church, but I was also more present and responsive at home. My wife and I experienced a measure of reconciliation. I joined the family for dinner each evening. I read bedtime stories to my girls, and then we "prayed through the day." I'd ask them if they remembered an event; they would giggle and say, "Yes," then we'd thank God for it. My illness would still cause me to hide in the cocoon of my study on occasion, but I stayed connected and together we were blessed.

Then, my wife's father became ill with colon cancer. I encouraged her to take the children and be there for him and her mom. She was reluctant, fearing I'd relapse. I told her I'd come up each Monday for a couple of days and assured her I'd be fine. It was a difficult decision, but I believe the best we could have made for all of us.

The church was growing, not exponentially, but steadily. There was a sense the Spirit was doing something new in our midst. We hired a dynamic music minister, Jeff Webb who infused light into the choir, leading them in songs from classical hymns to Negro Spirituals. We recruited a student pastor, David Perry. David was a Jewish-Christian rooted in sacred tradition with a passion for the LORD.

I was asked to chair the Committee on Preparation for Ministry (CPM). We oversaw students pursuing careers as pastors. It was a grueling process involving not only advanced academic work (including Greek and Hebrew), but rigorous spiritual self-examination, demonstrated interpersonal skills, and exhaustive psychological evaluation.

I attended a workshop for a group of CPM chairs. We studied training models, explored best practices, and brainstormed situations we were in or might encounter.

At one of these sessions, a young CPM chair remarked: *We have a student just diagnosed with bipolar disorder. How do we dismiss her quietly, so we don't set her off?*

I bit my tongue and listened as others asked questions. The woman was excelling academically. Her supervisors gave good evaluations and there were no red flags in her relationships. The only mark on her record was a mental health diagnosis.

Finally, I spoke, *It's essential we evaluate based on demonstrated behavior, not diagnostic codes. I have bipolar disorder myself yet I serve faithfully and fruitfully. Don't tell her she can't be a pastor; explore with her if this is her calling.*

~❖~

It never occurred to her to give up.

Kay Redfield Jamison

Jabez cried out to the God of Israel, Oh, that you would bless me and enlarge my territory! Let your hand be with me and keep me from harm so that I will be free from pain. And God granted his request.

1 Chronicles 4.10

CHAPTER FOURTEEN

maintenance remission

I was beating the odds. Proving my prognosis wrong. My ministry was strong. My marriage was intact. I was managing my illness with outpatient care. I was in my mid-thirties and had high hopes that my best days were still to come.

Still, I had a serious mental illness. No cure was on the horizon. Bipolar disorder, particularly rapid cycling, can upend your life when you least expect it. I hoped for the best, but prepared for the worst. I saw the glass not as half full or half empty, but as being consumed or poured out. I studied all I could about my illness, learned from the experience of others, and noted my own responses in incessant journals.

One thing I learned quickly and repeatedly is the strong genetic component of bipolar disorder. Armchair psychologists love to speculate and debate the nature vs. nurture question. One thing is certain -- numerous studies of parents with bipolar have shown that the child of a father with bipolar is 50% likely to have the gene. I had two children. You can do the math.

I made a difficult decision to get a vasectomy. I mention this not to overshare, but to better equip caregivers and others to be more compassionate about what persons with mental illness face.

Similar to certain genetic physical illnesses, some agonize over passing their suffering to the children. My decision was excruciating, though I tried to make light of it. I did not call on the spiritual, emotional, and relational help available and instead went through it alone.

In spite of this very real loss for me and my family, we were eager to grow. My wife's father had miraculously gone into remission. We were now home together again. Our life had become relatively stable. We believed we were ready for a leap of faith to better love God and others. My wife suggested foster care.

Over the next two years we fostered a dozen children on an emergency or transitional basis. Several came from homes with a parent who had mental illness. We didn't impose clinical language, but we talked openly about my moods and my need to be alone on occasion. This invited them to do the same when they felt overwhelmed. As with our biological children, they experienced an emotional honesty giving them a leg up on maturing in a stilted age.

I look back on those early days of my recovery and marvel both at how well I accepted my illness and how little I knew. My brain was like a sponge. I was soaking up information yet squeezing it out through no rhyme nor reason behavior. I would do something wise, then something foolish, my bipolar brain shaped my disordered life.

~❖~

It is always important to know when something has reached its end.
Closing circles, shutting doors, finishing chapters, it doesn't matter
what we call it; what matters is to leave in the past those moments in
life that are over.

Paulo Coelho

For I know the plans I have for you, declares the LORD, plans to pros-
per you and not to harm you, plans to give you hope and a future.

Jeremiah 29.11

~❖~

CHAPTER FIFTEEN

leaving well

Recently, I heard of a national journalist looking for stories from pastors who had been wrongfully persecuted when they were outed with mental illness. Certainly, these voices need to be heard. The church is called to be a compassionate community, and when we are not, we need to be called out on this.

But my story is nothing like this. My church lavished me and my family with steadfast support. Had they not done this at such a crucial moment in my life and ministry, I would have imploded. I would have lost my job, my home, my faith. The story of Cochranton Presbyterian Church and other faith communities like it needs to be told to show others what God can do when a congregation embraces a pastor or member with a mental illness and encourages that one to heal.

I've often asked myself -- if Cochranton was so wonderful to me, why did I leave after only four years? It certainly had nothing to do with the lack of faith in the people. No, there were three primary factors.

For one, we wanted to be closer to family. While my father-in-law's cancer had miraculously gone into remission, it had brought to light how much we wanted our children to grow up near grandparents. A church 15 miles from them expressed interest in me, so I made myself available for an interview.

Secondly, scoping out the church, I discovered they had an expansive outreach ministry -- a thrift shop, a food pantry, involvement at an addiction treatment center, and connections with two local prisons. I would be coming on board to provide spiritual support for existing programs, not having to create new ones.

And thirdly, things were going well in Cochranton, but I was sensing my mission there was nearing completion. The broad awareness that I was the "pastor with a mental illness," which had been instrumental in opening doors for ministry, was becoming more of a hindrance than a help. Many became lax in their own discipleship and, in doing so, also overlooked behavior I should have been held accountable for. We had come to a stasis of low expectations. I needed to test the waters, so I followed a path to the Finger Lakes region of New York for an interview.

The place God calls you to is the place where your deep gladness and the world's deep hunger meet.

Frederick Buechner

You have kept count of my tossings; put my tears in your bottle. Are they not in your record?

Psalm 56.8, NRSV

CHAPTER SIXTEEN

visiting linda

Only trust him if he is wearing cowboy boots. This was my first knowledge of the man who would become my supervisor for the next chapter of my ministry.

Sam Edwards was a man as short in stature as he was tall in grace and compassion. As long as I knew him, he always wore a beard. And cowboy boots.

When it became clear that I would receive a call to serve as pastor of Ovid Federated Church (OFC), I had an essential question to ask. I summoned up the courage to take Sam aside. *I have bipolar disorder. When and how should I disclose this?*

Sam asked me about the nature of my illness, how it impacted my behavior. He asked if I was compliant with medication and if I would be seeing a therapist. Then, he looked into the distance, as if computing the information I had just provided. He turned back to me and said something like:

You have no legal obligation to disclose. But for your own sake, I recommend you share it discreetly, first with two trusted leaders (naming two who worked as psychiatric nurses). As far as your pastoral role, follow the Spirit to open up when it contributes to better spiritual care.

Sam's advice turned out to be the best I have ever received about being a pastor with a mental illness. I would discover this the very next day.

I became aware of a young woman (I'll call Linda) who had been admitted to the psych unit of a nearby hospital. I checked with a family member to ask if I could pay her a visit. They were reluctant at first. Then I disclosed my own illness. I told them I had spent time in psych hospitals and knew how blessed I felt when a pastor visited. So they asked Linda for her permission and she granted it..

The psych unit was located at the far corner of the hospital. I had to walk through dark and dingy corridors to get there. I buzzed to get in and an aide opened the door, looking askance. She pointed to a room at the end of the hall.

I found Linda lying in bed with a sheet up to her chin, her leg exposed to reveal an open hospital gown.

Linda, I'm Pastor Tony. Thank you for letting me see you.

She lay completely still. I pulled up a chair beside her and sat in silence, listening for what the Spirit would say.

Linda, I don't know just what you are going through, but I do know what it's like to be in a dark valley. I've been in a place like this.

She turned to her side, facing me. I go on.

One thing I've discovered is that even in the darkest valleys, I've not been alone. Even though I felt like it at the time I was not alone. You are not alone, Linda. Do you know that?

A tear formed in the corner of her eye. I bowed my head and prayed, silently at first, then aloud:

Gracious God, you collect our tears in a bottle. You care for us more than we can possibly care for ourselves. Help Linda embrace your grace, in the Spirit of Jesus Christ.

She looked at me and through tears, quietly spoke. *Thank you for seeing me.*

Seeing and being seen are spiritual events. They only happen when two souls look through our circumstantial dividing walls and self-preserving masks and risk becoming one. When I looked into Linda's eyes and saw tears begin to melt her wounds, I shed a few of my own.

God anointed me with these tears to a renewed sense of calling, and to a place that would become not only my field of service, but my spiritual home.

The term "deinstitutionalization" conceals some simple truths, namely, that old, unwanted persons, formerly housed in state hospitals, are now housed in nursing homes; that young, unwanted persons, formerly also housed in state hospitals, are now housed in prisons or para-psychiatric facilities; and that both groups of inmates are systematically drugged with psychiatric medications.

Thomas Stephen Szasz

*You have searched me, L*ORD*, and you know me. You know when I sit and when I rise; you perceive my thoughts from afar. You discern my going out and my lying down; you are familiar with all my ways. Before a word is on my tongue you, L*ORD*, know it completely.*
You hem me in behind and before, and you lay your hand upon me.
Such knowledge is too wonderful for me,
too lofty for me to attain.

Psalm 139.1-6

CHAPTER SEVENTEENTH

asylums to prisons

When you google *Ovid, New York,* at the top of places to see, you'll find a unique tourist site:

> *Willard Asylum for the Chronic Insane: An abandoned asylum where patients have been forgotten but their possessions remain.*

The webpage gives a brief history:

> *Though asylums often carry connotations of dark and torturous existences, Willard and other institutions like it were intended to be a better alternative to systems in place for taking care of the mentally ill. In the early 19th century, those without anyone to care for them and incapable of taking care of themselves were left to almshouses (basically shelters) which were overcrowded and under-resourced. In response to these squalid conditions, New York's Surgeon General Dr. Sylvester D. Willard proposed a state-run hospital for the insane. Abraham Lincoln himself signed off on the proposal a mere six days before his death.*

Many of the people at Ovid Federated Church (OFC) had worked at Willard before the institution's final days, carrying a wide range of feelings and attitudes about mental healthcare and those in need of it. These same individuals were being asked to review the qualifications and trustworthiness of a prospective pastor with a serious mental illness. The two leaders with whom I confided had both been nurses at Willard. They were confident my diagnosis would not prevent me from faithful service. They concurred that I shouldn't have to keep it a secret, but simply use good judgement about when to open up.

The night before I was called as pastor, the church hosted a reception. I was seated at the table of one of the most soft-spoken saints in the church. His wife though was known to speak her mind. A tame tongue was not among her gifts. I got a sense of what challenges lie ahead when she said: *Yeah, they closed the asylum down then built a bunch of prisons for the bipolars and schizophrenics.*

I bit my tongue through a smile. I clenched my cheeks. Then I opened my mouth and started to speak. Right then someone asked me to return thanks for the meal. I was saved by grace.

So long as we love we serve; so long as we are loved by others, I would almost say that we are indispensable; and no man is useless while he has a friend.

Robert Louis Stevenson

Truly I tell you, whatever you did for one of the least of these brothers and sisters of mine, you did for me.

Matthew 25.40

CHAPTER EIGHTEENTH

village vicar

The village of Ovid, New York is nestled between two of the largest Finger Lakes. Cayuga points the way to left-leaning Ithaca where Cornell breeds Nobel Prize winners and hippie-hangers-on. The middle finger, Seneca, boasts vineyards and snowbird vacation homes who fly south for the winter. Ovid Federated Church (OFC) was a place where the two came together. In fact, when we were redoing the roof, the contractor coaxed me to climb the ladder, and from the top I could see the majesty of Seneca to the west and Cayuga to the north.

Ovid was a unique community in many ways. We were the home of college administrators, farmers, psychiatric nurses, small business owners, addiction counselors, teachers, and many with no vocational identity. All were both well represented and served at OFC.

At the thrift shop, where Esther, Dot, and Emma sorted and sold donated clothing. Everything was less than a dollar, including the underwear. At the ecumenical food pantry, we housed the space for the Holy Cross ladies to hand out a week's worth of groceries. The Scouts had a local chapter with us, and we came to know many boys and girls who found a safe haven in their troops.

Nearly all social services for the southside of Seneca County operated from our fellowship hall. The first Monday of each month,

I made a point of circling around, playing with children while their mothers picked up their W.I.C. checks.

Clients from Dick Van Dyke Addiction Treatment Center (ATC) worshipped with us, and I led a Monday morning Bible study there. Disabled veterans living at the Bixby home were integrated in ministry, as were residents of a home for those with developmental disabilities such as Down Syndrome.

I was the *Village Vicar*. The position came with great respect and much responsibility. I was invited into nearly everyone's lives, entrusted with stories about what they held dear, how they hurt, and who they loved (and hated). But this privilege came at a cost. I had no private life. Our house sat on the circle drive where people passed by on their way out of church. If you slowed down, you could see what we were having for dinner. If you were in need, you could ring the bell at any hour. Or, if you didn't want to wait, you would come on in.

Being Pastor Tony at OFC, I had nowhere to hide. My best and my worst were put on display for all to see. One of the leaders I respect a great deal summed up my ministry there very well:

When you were balanced, you were one of the best pastors I've known. And when you weren't, well... I'll leave it at that.

Discretion can be a blessed thing.

We tend to use prayer as a last resort, but God wants it to be our first line of defense. We pray when there's nothing else we can do, but God wants us to pray before we do anything at all.
Most of us would prefer, however, to spend our time doing something that will get immediate results. We don't want to wait for God to resolve matters in His good time because His idea of "good time" is seldom in sync with ours.

Oswald Chambers

But I cry to you for help, LORD; in the morning my prayer comes before you.

Psalm 88.13

CHAPTER NINETEEN

morning prayer

The first decade of my ministry had been strangled by the "tyranny of the urgent." Rather than steadfastly advancing in God's kingdom work, I was in steady retreat, tossing up desperate pleas for deliverance rather than confident prayers for victory. When I accepted the call to serve as pastor of OFC, I was determined to move past this. So, taking a page out of my St. Luke's playbook, I established a time for morning prayer in the chapel. We read through the Scriptures, lifted up praise, confessed our sins, gave thanks, asked God to bless others, and prayed for God to guide our mission and ministry.

At first we met in the front of the sanctuary, but the setting was too vast for a small group, so I turned my office into a chapel for prayer and study. There was room for a dozen or so, and we never had too many or too few. Every weekday at 8 am, people could count on the fact that the chapel would be open, prayers would be said, and that the Spirit would be with the two or three or twelve present, interceding on behalf of their needs.

Morning prayer benefited my ministry in many ways. On a personal level, it got me out of bed each day. Some days it was all I could do to drag myself to the chapel. I would keep my head bowed, more out of despondency than reverence. I would say the Scripture verses assigned and maybe the names of those requesting or highlighted for prayer. Rather than spiritual fervor, I showed a flat affect and felt not the least moved by the Spirit. But I was there, with God's people, in the name of Christ. God was listening, not because of what a dynamic pastor I was, but because I was being a faithful shepherd, leading the flock in the right paths, for his name's sake.

Two among the flock became prayer warriors for me and our ministry. Donalee Kelly was an unassuming grandmother with a non-anxious presence. Her ability to listen without interjection or judgement made her a trusted counselor for many, including me.

Then there was Bill Robenolt. I had been introduced to Bill by his therapist. Bill had the desire to be involved in a church but was reluctant due to his peculiar mannerisms. Bill lived with schizophrenia, talking to people others couldn't see and laughing at jokes others didn't hear. Sometimes he stood up and walked out as if someone told him to leave.

I encouraged Bill to come to morning prayer, thinking it would be a gateway to broader involvement. The first day he showed up I asked if he would read a Scripture verse. I discovered he had a very dynamic voice drawing attention to the Word. He soon became a key liturgist and a much loved member of the faith fellowship.

The structure and substance of morning prayer helped maintain my relative stability. As a pastor, it's easy to fall into the trap of doing only what is demanded or creating more work for yourself than is needed. God set my day's agenda at morning prayer. Rather than constantly retreating, I confidently pressed forward, facing head-on urgent tasks that otherwise held me hostage.

~❖~

Christian life is not a life divided between times for action and times for contemplation. No. Real social action is a way of contemplation, and real contemplation is the core of social action.

Henri J.M. Nouwen

The boundary lines have fallen for me in pleasan places; surely, I have a delightful inheritance.

Psalm 16.6

CHAPTER TWENTIETH

passionate pursuits

While prayer shaped my days at Ovid Federated Church (OFC), I did not remain in a prayer closet for any length of time. In addition to preparing sermons, I led Bible studies, coached folks through crisis, advised ministry teams to plan worship, conducted outreach, promoted fellowship, and engaged in stewardship. All the sorts of things a solo pastor is charged to do, whether s/he is equipped or not.

I also officiated weddings and funerals within and beyond the church. I viewed these as my biggest opportunities for evangelism, and there were many. One Saturday alone, I led four funerals and a wedding. In each service, I tried to inject the Good News that in life and in death we belong to God. It didn't concern me so much how many came to church after these events, as whether I had faithfully shared the love of Christ that shapes our lives together and gives us hope for the life to come.

Not everything I did was sacred. I participated in several secular pursuits. A church member, Dave Griffith, invited me to join him attending the high school basketball games at South Seneca. The Falcons were perennial state title contenders and the whole town was swept up in the fervor for the sport. From the opening tip to the final buzzer, I was transfixed, reliving Hoosier Hysteria. My competitive drive brought out the best and the worst in me. I would go from cheering jubilantly over a great shot to jeering sharply at the referees for a botched call. I could not contain either my enthusiasm when things went my way or sense of injustice when they didn't..

I have served in other ministry settings where I was expected to always be completely contained when on display for others. This aggravated my mental well-being, as my disordered mind refuses to be tamed. My only option was to go into hiding, and this isolation produced shame upon shame. The people of Ovid, not even aware of my diagnosis, extended to me the latitude to be human. And not just human, but one with great passions loudly expressed. I was able to be emotionally honest and show psychological integrity, moving forward in mission with pleasant delight.

~❖~

Look to the living, love them, and hold on.

Kay Redfield Jamison

O God, who gave us birth, you are ever more ready to hear than we
are to pray. You know our needs before we ask, and our ignorance in
asking. Show us now your grace, that as we face the mystery of death
we may see the light of eternity. Speak to us once more your solemn
message of life and of death. Help us to live as those who are prepared to
die. And when our days here are ended, enable us to die as those
who go forth to live,
so that living or dying, our life may be in
Jesus Christ our risen LORD. Amen.
Book of Common Worship Daily Prayer

CHAPTER TWENTY-ONE

denise on a mission

One of my biggest fears in seminary was leading youth ministry. This fear was aggravated in a Field Education position where I was expected to design and direct a program in which adults and youth worked together to carry out meaningful ministry. Such a cross-generational approach is a perfect model but the distance between ideal perfection and harsh reality is vast. I failed mostly because when an adult mentor and a youth member didn't form a faithful bond, I took it personally. I became enmeshed with the young person and my gut wrenched, feeling I had been abandoned.

My crass self says parents want youth pastors to do what they refuse to do, relate to their children. Yet, I know now it's much more than this. The years since seminary shaved away some of my cynicism. I had become a parent myself, and the log in my own eye kept me from picking at splinters in the eyes of others. At Ovid, I came to know many desperate parents who wanted more than anything to care for their wounded children, and, in spite of their best efforts, they needed help.

The best opportunities I had to serve in ministry together with youth and adults was mission trips. Thanks to the tireless efforts of such leaders as Priscilla Smalser, Pat & Betsy Sayer, Dean & Patti Arcangeli, Jim & Marcia Klue, Ralph Reigle, and others, I was able to go on two youth mission trips to Washington, D.C. and one to Philadelphia. Leaving behind familiar masks, we joined God at work in the world and learned how much we desperately depended on our Father in heaven.

The number of details required to make for a meaningful mission trip for over twenty persons boggled my mind. Partnering with an agency. Recruiting, team building, fundraising, communication, transportation. Even one aspect of these would have overwhelmed me. But it never came to this. All I had to do was focus on my role in providing pastoral care and counsel. I could do what I was called to do and it would be enough.

We faced tremendous challenges those three years. Perhaps the most traumatic was when the friend of one of our youth had come along on the trip. I'll call her Denise. Things had been going awry early in the week and tensions were high. The girls were all sleeping on one floor of an old building that was quite dingy. Given the parameters of our contract, there wasn't much we could do about it. The pressure kept building. Relationships were strained. Emotions were high.

One morning Patti took me aside. Denise had been up all night scrubbing floors with a toothbrush, humming hymns. The other girls were spooked. Patti tried to comfort her, encouraging her to rest, but Denise was in a trance.

We agreed on a strategy to surround her with caring attention and monitor her behavior. It was good Patti was a school nurse and Priscilla a psych nurse. Between the two, they saw Denise was safe and the others were not impacted more than they had to be. Thankfully, Denise calmed down and rejoined the group.

About a year later I received word that Denise had taken her own life. She became so fixated with being clean that her mind convinced her death would be the only pure sacrifice acceptable to the LORD.

As I share this story, my hands shake. Was there something more we could have done? Should we have stopped her from going on this mission trip? Should we have taken her to a psych hospital? Should we have done some sort of spiritual intervention?

Yet, even with shaky hands, my mind says for certain that given the situation, there was nothing more to do. As much as we want someone to choose life, we can't always prevent suicide. It is a tragedy and a truth that someone whose mind has betrayed them may take this extreme measure to stop the pain. It's not your fault. IT'S NOT YOUR FAULT! Tell yourself that over and over again until it sinks in. And rest assured that nothing in life or in death separates us from the love of God in Christ, not even death by our own hands.

Studies show that suicide rates among young people have sky-rocketed over the past decade. Suicide is the second leading cause of death for 15-24 year olds. If we are to offer hope, we need to share purpose. Our OFC trips did that. Youth engaged in mean-ingful missions alongside caring faithful adults. We did the best we could do.

Until there is a cure for mental illness, no amount of infused hope will be able to prevent suicide. In our actions, we can sup-port scientific research toward this end. By faith, we carry and share the hope that life is worth living and that death is not the final word.

Be not angry that you cannot make others as you wish them to be, since you cannot make yourself as you wish to be.

Thomas à Kempis

But I, through the abundance of your steadfast love, will enter your house, I will bow down toward your holy temple in awe of you. Lead me, O Lord, in your righteousness because of my enemies; make your way straight before me.

Psalm 5.7-8

CHAPTER TWENTY-TWO

maintaining mental health

I continued my own therapeutic care. I found a psychiatrist in Ithaca known as a top-notch prescriber. Dr. Gunn navigated me through a vast array of medication changes such that I maintained relative balance. She understood my need to continue in full-time work, yet also kept her eye on my long-term prognosis. She was conservative in changes made and gave me strategies for self-care to keep me out of the hospital.

I also found Mitch Bobrow, a therapist in Ithaca, who strengthened my psychological safety net. Using a variety of treatment methods, many of which I had learned in seminary, he gave me tools to understand my life story so I could better shape my own narrative moving forward.

Though steeped in a Judeo-Christian worldview, Mitch had become a practicing Buddhist. He did not impose his faith perspective on me but used it to sharpen my own faith. In session, he would bring up stories from the Hebrew Scriptures and parables of Jesus to engage me as I reflected on my own story. When I hid behind theology concept to avoid facing reality, he'd call me out on it.

People often ask me if they should only see a Christian counselor, and I used to say an emphatic YES! After having Mitch as a therapist, I've tempered my response. Good therapists are cognizant of and respectful of our faith convictions, but they need not share them.

In addition to clinical care, my personal and pastoral safety nets were strengthened by pastors in the community and servant leaders in the church. One pastor, Tom Lange, was a great mentor of mine. He gave me some of the best advice I've ever received for ministry leadership -- *Don't try to change people to be more like you. Instead, love them into mutual transformation.*

This counsel has served me well.. When I beat people over the head with *I'm Mentally Ill, Accept Me!* I fail miserably and the stigma increases.But when I self disclose, *I love you and I have a mental illness*, more often than not change happens. Stigma may not disappear, but it dissipates.

Looking back at journals while I served OFC (1994-2006), I marvel at how I served as effectively as I did. We experienced significant growth according to nearly all ministry measures, materially and spiritually. I officiated over 200 funerals and countless weddings, balanced with fathering four children; all without needing in-patient treatment or hospitalization. How? By the grace of God. Not generic grace, but grace working through the body of Christ, people of the church:

- People like Carol Limner, our Board chair and first person I told of my diagnosis. From disclosure forward, Carol never betrayed my trust. She respected my pastoral authority yet wasn't afraid to lovingly confront me when necessary.

- Paul McPherson, the local funeral director. While not an OFC member, Paul was a trusted colleague often coaching me through peculiar family situations in such a way I could better share the Good News of life beyond this life in Christ.

- Laurie Butler, our administrative assistant. While I did not formally share my diagnosis with her until well into my tenure, she had a strong spiritual intuitiveness often filling much-needed gaps to my blind spots while I served OFC.

These and many others made my pastorate in Ovid fruitful and fulfilling. Perhaps if I stayed, I would have enjoyed both ongoing spiritual growth and psychological stability. But maybe not. I may have crashed and been unable to keep myself and my family afloat. While the LORD's love for us is steadfast, it is perhaps the only thing in life that is.

My analysis of hundreds of cases of occupational incompetence led me to formulate The Peter Principle: "In a Hierarchy Every Employee Tends to Rise to His Level of Incompetence."

Laurence J. Peter

Trust in the LORD with all your heart and lean not on your own understanding; in all your ways submit to him, and he will make your paths straight.

Proverbs 3.5-6

CHAPTER TWENTY-THREE

peter principle

In seminary, we were warned not to quest for success. Within my denomination, 60% of churches have less than 100 members. That's on the rolls. If you look out from the pulpit on any given Sunday, you might see, at best 50 steadfast souls, barely enough to warm the pews. Such numbers are discouraging for many ministers serving small churches. It is little wonder the average length of stay in pastorates is now less than four years.

My head knew all these things. And my heart wanted to stay in Ovid as long as they would have me. Yet some other part of my being became restless. I wanted more. Not just more money, but more opportunities and more challenges. Just more. So I put aside all of the faith convictions that brought me to Ovid and cast my net in deeper waters.

On an island in the ocean, in fact -- Long Island. In a former potato patch that became a bedroom community for the Big Apple. The village of Greenlawn is just a one-hour commute by rail to Grand Central Station. From there you were a short subway ride from professions that would fulfill your wildest dreams, the longing of many.

Greenlawn Presbyterian was filled with such longing. Not just in a material sense, but in a true and spiritual one. The people I met on the Pastor Search Committee were people who loved the

LORD and wanted what was best for their church. They were honest about the challenges. The church had once had over 1,000 members, and now it was down to less than 200. They didn't consciously expect a new pastor to restore them to former glory, but . . . the hopes and fears of all those years were kept in one who would do so. Deep down, they wanted a pastor who could save them. I wanted to save them. We both needed the Savior. Instead we got each other.

Leaving Ovid was very much like facing the death of a loved one. I was taught in ministry that when you leave a pastorate, you cut all ties with former members so they can bond with their new ministers. I violated this once and was called on the carpet such that I knew it was not a casual recommendation, but a cardinal sin. How could I leave the people who had helped hone my pastoral skills, raise my children, and maintain my mental health?

One of the last funerals I officiated at Ovid was for Art Burdin. Art was a tall, lanky man, a Cornell alum who had served his family, church, and community for well over 80 years and was ready to rest in peace. I was there when he took his last breath, and I can attest there was a gentle smile on his face. Art and others like him showed that in life and in death, we belong to God.

DESCENDING INTO THE PIT

To say goodbye is to die a little.

Raymond Chandler

Folly is an unruly woman; she is simple and knows nothing. She sits at the door of her house, on a seat at the highest point of the city, calling out to those who pass by, who go straight on their way, "Let all who are simple come to my house!" To those who have no sense she says, "Stolen water is sweet; food eaten in secret is delicious!" But little do they know that the dead are there, that her guests are deep in the realm of the dead.

Proverbs 9.13-18

CHAPTER TWENTY-FOUR

death of pride

My move from Ovid to Long Island was like a death in many ways. In my brief time at Greenlawn, I would die a thousand deaths. The first death began with a funeral. The moment I landed, I became aware that a life-long pillar of the church had died. Pastorally, I felt I needed to walk with the family through their grief. I did just this; but I did more than this. Rather than walk alongside them, leading the way to the Good Shepherd, I began a personal quest to become their only beloved shepherd, drawing their attention away from Christ and to myself. It took the life out of me and almost took my life permanently.

I replaced my commitments to God and to my family with an all-consuming drive to rescue the church from itself, from the community around them, and from the Enemy who prowls throughout the world to snatch us. I'm not sure how I intended to do this, and I never spent enough time in prayer to discover how God could do it through me. Truthfully, I'm not sure exactly what I did with my days, but I know I would often leave the house as early as 3 am, walk the mile and a half to church, do ministry throughout the day and arrive home as late as 11 pm.. I did this for over a year.

I'd like to think I made a difference in some people's lives, and, to be fair, I trust I did -- by the grace of God. There was a man, a recovering addict, who rooted his faith in a Higher Power to a relationship with Jesus Christ. Another man wandered into the church one day, not knowing what he was looking for, and I discovered that he was a disabled veteran struggling with major depression who essentially had become a hermit. I encouraged him to meet with me weekly for conversation and prayer. He did. Eventually he would come to worship and join the church. There were two women on fire for the mission of Scouts. They approached me about the church becoming a charter organization. I was impressed by their deep faith and passion to nurture young lives. I helped them navigate the process and in return, they would look to me as an unofficial chaplain of the group -- a spiritual mentor for the youth and guide for their parents and troop leaders.

But for every divine victory I would take part in, there were countless losses. I won't belabor you or depress myself with details. Suffice it to say I committed the greatest sin, the root of all sins -- pride. And more than just garden valley pride; it was the sort of pride where I tried to take the place of God. I was even prideful in my humility, hoping not so much that I would point to Christ, but that people would see me as a perfect reflection of Christ -- a subtle but crucial distinction.

One aspect of this pride is that I foolishly opted not to disclose my mental illness. Perhaps I had a good reason. For one, the community was not the sort of culture that nourished the weak. Long Island brought the ethos of Manhattan home. It fostered a cutthroat culture where only the strongest survived. Parents would not want their children to be around folks with flaws that might prevent them from greatness. This reality hit close to home one year at our Living Nativity. My son, who has Down syndrome, wandered around the village scene and wound up at the manger, kneeling beside the baby Jesus. While many were deeply moved by his Christ-like faith, others complained that he stole the show and ruined the spirit of the occasion.

The church, or at least the unspoken mission of the church was to create the best faith community that would bolster healthy families toward success. There was little room for a spiritual leader to have personal flaws, particularly one as debilitating as mental illness. So I kept my mouth shut. Until my mind refused to be silenced.

~❖~

The man who kills a man kills a man.
The man who kills himself kills all men.
As far as he is concerned, he wipes out the world.

G.K. Chesterton

Then the devil took [Jesus] to the holy city and had him stand on the
highest point of the temple. If you are the Son of God, [Satan] said,
throw yourself down. For it is written:
"He will command his angels concerning you,
and they will lift you up in their hands,
so that you will not strike your foot against a stone."
Jesus answered him, It is also written:
"Do not put the Lord your God to the test.

Matthew 4.5-7

CHAPTER TWENTY-FIVE

(near) death of self

I never wanted to kill myself, even as I was swallowing enough pills to accomplish the feat. It happened like this.

I was walking home from church one chilly Saturday night. I had just finished preparing my sermon, and my mind was racing forward to various ministry matters that I wanted to take care of as Easter approached. Suddenly, a sharp wind took my breath away. I became flush; my bones ached. I thought it was the early on-set of the flu. By the time I got home, I felt awful. Thinking I might be contagious, I called someone to lead worship the next day.

It was only about 8 pm, but I said goodnight to my wife and children and went to bed. I can't remember if I even changed my clothes. I closed my eyes. My head hurt. My joints throbbed. I felt miserable. And then, my dark misery was replaced by a desperate mission.

I heard a voice from the corner of the ceiling,

It's okay.

I looked around the room. No one was there. I heard the voice again. I looked in the hall. Nobody.

It's okay.

Had I been in my right mind, I would have heard this as reassurance from God that in spite of my struggles, all would be well. This is not what I heard. Instead, I believed God was giving me permission to kill myself, and that this would somehow be a final solution to not only my problems, but to those of my family, the church, and the world.

I acted with haste, opened my drawer and took out the two most potent medications I had. I popped hands full of these into my mouth, not measuring their lethal effectiveness. I only acted on a voice I believed was God's. Now I know it was the deceiver who, though not having the power to kill us, has the power of suggestion to prompt us to kill ourselves.

The next thing I knew it was over a day later. I came in and out of a fog. My wife pieced together the story for me. She found me bent over on the floor of my bedroom, body stiff. She contacted my psychiatrist, who said she didn't need to call an ambulance but rather just watch me through the night. So she did.

I was seething with anger. Angry at myself for not completing the task. Angry at my wife for not leaving me alone. Angry at God for rescuing me for some ungodly reason. In the strength of this anger, I pushed through the days ahead, discovering in time a reason to live.

My method of dealing with depression was not to lash out but to retreat. When I was depressed, I would curl up on our bed and sleep. I could sleep at any time of the day or night, and sleep soundly for hours. I would avoid the family, in part because the noise was so painful to me that I could not stand it and in part because I did not want to make others miserable by my presence. I did not understand at that time that my family and friends truly missed me. I later came to realize this and moved my nest from our bed to the living room as I improved. I was silent and still unable to move, but at least I was there, with the children and my husband.

Kathryn Greene-McCreight

*You have taken from me friend and neighbor
darkness is my closest friend.*

Psalm 88.18

CHAPTER TWENTY-SIX

death of identity

God rescued me from death, then stripped away what was my life. After my overdose, I spent three weeks in the psych unit of Columbia Presbyterian hospital. There, with help of caring aides, nurses, therapists, doctors, and others I regained a sense that life was worth living.

Shortly after I returned home from the hospital, I was encouraged to accept a disability package from my employer. My supervisor did not think I would survive in pastoral ministry with my illness. On one hand, disability was a blessing, providing a measure of financial security to live modestly while focusing on my well-being. On the other hand, it robbed me of my identity. I had come to view my ministry as my connection with God and I feared that if I lost that, I would lose God as well.

The first step we had to take was to move off Long Island. We found a farmhouse thirty miles from my wife's parents with seven acres. I suppose the thinking was that I could rehabilitate by living off the land. Nice in theory, but, as some have said, I'm allergic to work. I admire those who find joy and purpose living off the land, but I'm not one of them. The more I tried to work the garden, paint fence posts, and do odd jobs, the more depressed I became and couldn't bring myself to do them.

Depression became my constant companion. I took to my bed, not so much to sleep as stare at the walls and search them for signs of what I could do with my future. The walls did not speak. I tried some volunteer work at the VA, and, at first, I enjoyed the moments interacting with those who had more reason to be depressed than I did. But engaging with veterans offered only temporary relief. As soon as I left them, I drove home in darkness, unable to conceive of what to do with the rest of the week.

I was having to reinvent myself from nothing, and I lacked inspiration. One step I took in an effort to discover something new was to attend worship at an Anabaptist church. I came to respect the people there a great deal. They welcomed me warmly. One man took me to work with him where I was able to enjoy companionship and do something productive. Another met with me weekly for Bible study and fellowship. We were often invited to people's homes for Sunday dinner and conversation. Though I was still in a depressive stupor, I felt a measure of relief being around Christ followers who cared about me even though they didn't understand my illness.

Fellowship with others, though, would not lift me out of my pit and I began to wonder if it was a pit of my own making. Maybe the doctors were wrong about my diagnosis. Maybe I wasn't depressed so much as I was lazy. Maybe with some imposed discipline, I could get a kick-start that would be just what I needed to reform.

I became aware of a program near Lancaster, Pennsylvania that was described as a "Discipleship Center." It had originally been designed to help released prisoners acclimate to society and re-enter their families as spiritual heads. When they couldn't get ex-inmates to enroll, they shifted their focus on men like me who wanted some form of behavioral modification. I desperately wanted to become the family man I had not been and they provided an answer. I didn't pause to consider what it would cost me.

When I arrived at the Discipleship Center, I was made to sign a paper forgoing all my personal rights to make life decisions. I would be denied all contact with family or friends for three months. Then I could only have one 15 minute phone call with my wife each week.. My mail, outgoing and incoming, would be opened and examined. Any concerning issues would be discussed in "counseling sessions." I was only allowed to read a King James Version of the Bible or titles from an Anabaptist press. I had to follow the schedule that was set for me, moment by moment. I even had to ask to go to the bathroom (and urinated on myself several times before getting permission.)

Why did I sign up for this? Simply put, I wanted to be transformed into the spiritual head I was being taught to be. I desperately desired this narrow vision of what it meant to be a good husband, a faithful father, a submissive servant of the Lord. I saw no other way to do this on my own, so I accepted a radical approach from people who presented it as the answer to all my problems; the only Christian way. I allowed them to strip my personal freedom and dignity in some vain hope that it would restore my mind, my body, and my spirit. Strangely enough, it worked, but not the way they intended it.

After ten months apart from my family, they brought my wife down for a series of marital counseling sessions. These sessions, rather than a mutual examination of our relationship, became grueling psychological warfare as six persons, my wife included, tore apart my psyche. It was excruciating. If I ever wanted to kill myself, it was then.

Then something snapped. My inquisitors began to question my fitness to have ever been a pastor. My wife spoke up, *Well, I had to write his sermons for him.*

That was it. You could question my sanity, but you could not question my ability as a writer. It was then that I knew I had to escape the bondage that kept me from delighting in the Lord.

~❖~

DEVELOPING A PLAN

There are as many worlds as there are kinds of days, and as an opal changes its colors and its fire to match the nature of a day, so do I.

John Steinbeck

*Your word is a lamp for my feet,
a light on my path.*

Psalm 119.105

CHAPTER TWENTY-SEVEN

leaving home

After ten months at the Discipleship Center, I was given leave to visit home for two weeks. But the home I returned to was not a welcoming place to be. In just a few days, an inner conviction grew inside me that I had to escape the oppressive weight bearing down on me, even if it meant leaving home. But I knew no good way out, so I followed desperate measures to launch into an unknown future. It went like this:

- I sold my childhood baseball cards for a used bicycle.

- One Sunday, I rode my bike to a church I'd never visited.

- I asked one of the men to take me to the psych hospital.

- I was evaluated and found capable of being released.

- I begged staff to find room for me at a homeless shelter.

- They refused, saying, *They would eat you alive.*

- I contacted Sam Edwards for guidance.

- Sam referred me to a local church with an outreach program.

- The church fed me and put me up in a motel.

- My parents sent money to last until I could get my own.

- I found an attic apartment for a good price.

- I moved in with my bike, dishes, clothes, and journals.

I have many regrets about leaving my family in this way. I wish I had conceived a better option. But I've come to accept that we make the best decisions we can with the knowledge we have at the time, and trust God will take care of the rest. Launching out on my own was perhaps the most difficult thing I've ever done in my life. But I fully believed, and still believe, that the only way I could maintain my identity and my sanity was to leave. I might have been running away, but I think more likely I was running toward a path God had chosen for me. A path that would lead to healing, for myself and for others.

Home is the place where, when you have to go there, They have to take you in.

Robert Frost

The Lord is exalted over all the nations, his glory above the heavens. Who is like the Lord our God,
the One who sits enthroned on high, who stoops down to look on the heavens and the earth? He raises the poor from the dust and lifts the needy from the ash heap; he seats them with princes, with the princes of his people. He settles the childless woman in her home as a happy mother of children. Praise the Lord.

Psalm 113.4-9

CHAPTER TWENTY-EIGHT

finding my vocation

My parents divorced when I was 11. Over the next 40 years, I lived in 22 different places. I was a wandering soul in search of a home I could call my own.

After leaving the Discipleship Center, I went to Rochester, New York. Though there only three months, I found support from the saints at Grace church. Pastor Marc Swan invited me into fellowship. I was nurtured in the Word by Carl Schauffle. I was encouraged in my walk with Christ by Peter and Chris Mason. Grace provided me a sense of spiritual stability, helping me gain confidence that I had the faith to press on. But, apart from Sundays, I had nothing to shape my week. I grew restless and decided to move back to Indiana.

I found an apartment in Indianapolis. Being lonely I easily fell into a toxic relationship with a woman who was carrying wounds even deeper than mine. As in my days at Long Island, I tried to be a savior. I failed many times. When the burden of my failures became too much to bear, I escaped to Columbus, moving in with my father and step-mom.

Columbus is known for its architecture and God rebuilt my life there in a beautiful way. I began writing daily, composing well over a thousand words each day. I ate well, took long walks, and cared for the family dog. I also found a wonderful therapist and skilled psychiatrist. Though I had debilitating bouts of depression, they didn't last long. The thrill of manic episodes were well contained thanks in large part to my sister April, a psych nurse.

On April 5 of 2013, my sense of meaning and purpose crystalized when I learned of Matthew Warren's death by suicide. Matthew was the son of Rick Warren, pastor of Saddleback church, author of *The Purpose-Driven Life*. Matthew's death ignited in me an urgent drive to engage in mental health ministry more fully, thrusting myself into it as I once did pastoral ministry.

How did Warren's death spark such motivation? For one, it was the gross misunderstanding of mental illness displayed by so many within and beyond the church. Critics from the left and right seized on the opportunity to stomp on grief. Some said that the death was God's judgement on Warren's watered-down theology; others claimed that Matthew was questioning his sexual identity and his parents rejected him.

Such sinful speculation infuriated me. Rick and his wife Kay seemed to handle this with grace and would come through such persecution with endurance and hope for those of us who, like Matthew, are afflicted with brain diseases even to the point of death.

Writing has always been my best form of therapy. After Matthew died, it would become my primary vocation.

Countless times, when I have been driven to the edge of a cliff, God has rescued me and set me on level ground. Why would God do this? Because God delights in me, even in my disorder.

Tony Roberts

Take delight in the Lord,
and he will give you the desires of your heart.

Psalm 37.4

CHAPTER TWENTY-NINE

delight in disorder

Throughout the course of my ministry, I have reflected deeply on the *Psalms*. Often my morning prayer would consist of reading a Psalm, picking out a verse or two, then writing a devotion relating it to my life. I did some of this in a now-defunct blog, and it had been well received. Now with the impetus of creating a better understanding of faith and mental illness, I set out to write a book of such devotions.

One of the best God-led decisions I made during this time was to recruit a good editor -- Leanne Sype. Leanne would become not only an editor, but an encourager, a publishing coordinator, a fundraiser, and a good friend. Leanne helped shape the disorder of my dilapidated mind into a house that made beautiful sense.

My initial hope was that a traditional publisher would pick it up, but they didn't. Independent publishers (what some call "vanity presses") were eager to snatch up the manuscript and publish it for thousands of dollars, but Leanne and others steered me in an alternative direction -- self-publishing with a team of dedicated partners. Technology has now made it possible for an author to produce a book that rivals what traditional publishers could do. Self-publishers make all creative decisions and could obtain copies of their books for a good value.

From April of 2013 to March of 2014, I devoted several hours each day to writing, re-writing, and shaping what would become my first book, *Delight in Disorder: Ministry, Madness, Mission.* We estimated the cost of publication and held a successful crowd-funding campaign. Leanne recruited Nicole Miller, a graphic designer for the book cover and campaign video. We got Christina Tarabouchi from Ashberry Press to do the formatting. Smashwords did the ebook and Ingram Sparks the printing. In the afternoon of March 14, 2014, the UPS man came to my door with five boxes of books -- hot off the press. And not a moment too soon, as I had a book signing at the Bartholomew County Public Library that evening where I spoke to a gathering of over one hundred persons. It was a momentous occasion. Thank God I was manic or I might have missed it.

DESIGNING A PARTNERSHIP

Friendship ... is born at the moment when one man says to another "What! You too? I thought that no one but myself .

C.S. Lewis

*How good and pleasant it is
when God's people live together in unity!*

Psalm 133.1

eric riddle | 117

CHAPTER THIRTY

eric riddle

Eric Riddle is a man of many gifts. He is a compassionate father, a faithful church member, a tireless volunteer, and much more. He also has bipolar disorder, and when I met him this is what was dominating his life. He had recently become unemployed due in large part to his illness. His depression was getting the best of him, and his wife Jen was deeply concerned for his well-being. When she saw a newspaper article featuring my book signing, she urged Eric to contact me. He did and in a booth one day at Jill's Diner, we launched a friendship that would endure many highs and lows over the six years, with no signs of letting up.

First we agreed to meet weekly for conversation and prayer. There would be no agenda, just listening to each other and to God. We would walk through his neighborhood, searching for divine guidance as to how we could receive the support we needed and how we could share this support with others. We agreed a key component of this support needed to be spiritual. We both had experience in group therapy that was beneficial, but only in a limited way. Building interpersonal relationships improve communication techniques, but only faith can give us meaningful connections with God, self, and others.

What if we formed a faith-based mental health support group that included spiritual practices such as prayer, Scripture reading, and a time of silence, with more secular ones such as an educational component and a time for sharing? We researched models such as *NAMI Faith Net*, *Mental Health Grace Alliance*, and the work David Zucker was doing at University Presbyterian in Seattle. We quickly gained the sense that faith-based mental health support groups were few and far between, and we would be filling a much-needed void -- for ourselves and others. It took nine months after conception to give birth to a faith-based weekly support group we called *Faithful Friends*.

Before we gathered for our first meeting, we interviewed various pastors and community leaders to gain a sense of who might benefit from such a ministry. Eric and I agreed that if only the two of us showed up, it would be worthwhile. Still, we personally invited some we knew had a mental illness, hoping we might have a small group that would foster discussion and better promote healing.. Eight people attended our first gathering. We have maintained this average on a weekly basis, with people coming according to various factors such as geography, perceived need, and perhaps some group dynamics.

We now head into a new decade with challenges, but strengths to serve. The current pandemic has forced us into physical isolation. We still meet in Zoom, but this inhibits intimate sharing and we have lost members and momentum. Who knows what lies ahead, but I am confident that the God who began in us a good work will carry it through to completion.

I'm convinced the best way to break out of the prison of misery caused by mental illness is through building faith relationships. People with bipolar or other mental illnesses don't need an overabundance of mental health professionals, but we do need plenty of faithful friends.

Tony Roberts

I no longer call you servants, because a servant does not know his master's business. Instead, I have called you friends, for everything that I learned from my Father I have made known to you.

John 15.15

~❖~

CHAPTER THIRTY-ONE

faithful friends

Faithful Friends is a support group for persons with a mental illness and their invited loved ones. It is peer-led and faith-based. These are our guidelines:

We are a safe group: We recognize the volatility of mental health struggles. When someone is experiencing elevated symptoms, we may gently provide one-on-one support to determine the best course of action. Leaders have the right to contact clinical providers and family members when concerned for the health of an individual.

We are a peer-led group: Peers encourage other peers and provide each other with a vital sense of mutually supportive relationships, valued roles, and community. When we think that our own life experience might be helpful to the person speaking, we offer (but never insist) to share the lessons we've learned.

We are not a clinical group: We are not professional psychiatrists, psychologists, or social health workers. We may discuss our own medication experiences or encourage discussing medicine changes with doctors, but we do not suggest what medicine is best for another individual. We encourage talk therapy as a valuable component of the recovery process.

We are a wellness group: Wellness is a conscious, self-directed, and evolving process of achieving full potential. Physical, social, emotional, occupational, intellectual, and spiritual well-being are all addressed as part of a holistic lifestyle that everyone can pursue.

We practice spiritual disciplines: Our aim is to display Christ-like hospitality to children of God from all walks of life and diverse faith backgrounds. We draw on resources of prayer, Scripture, personal testimony, and fellowship. Our goal is to inspire and affirm others with hope and love.

We are not a church: We do not function as professional clergy and are neither authorized nor desire to take the place of a faith community. Our aim is to compliment an individual's walk of faith so that he or she will be inspired to seek out and grow within a spiritual body.

We are an accountability group: We are honest with ourselves and others. We set goals for ourselves that are specific, measurable, attainable, realistic, and timely (SMART). We check in with each other to see if we are working towards meeting our goals. We do not tell others how to fix their problems, nor do we expect others to solve our problems.

We are a confidential group: Though we are not bound by HIPAA rules, we do respect an individual's privacy. Conversations during a meeting are not discussed with non-leaders absent from the meeting and vice versa. The only exception to this rule is if someone is planning to harm themselves or others.

We are a respectful group: We listen empathetically. Please silence cell phones. Side discussions, flirting, and inappropriate commenting are discouraged. If someone is too distractive, s/he may be asked to step away from the group. Disrespectful commenting on the secret Faithful Friends Facebook page will not be permitted.

We are a fun group: Socializing outside the group is encouraged. With consent, phone numbers and/or email addresses are shared. Parties, social events, and invitations to faith communities are great ways to build friendships outside the meetings.

We are an inclusive group: We respect the diversity of persons in the group, and refrain from criticizing another's spiritual views, even when they differ from our own. We do not make disparaging remarks about another's race, ethnicity, gender, mental health diagnosis, or sexual identity.

We are a responsive group: The leadership team welcomes your questions, concerns, and ideas. Call or email us to talk or set up a meeting.

With these guidelines in place, we following this agenda:

1. **Opening Prayer:** *said by a volunteer*

2. **Announcements:** *shared by leaders*

3. **Guidelines:** *read in circle, leader highlights one*

4. **Introductions:** *name and something fun like,* "If you were a candy bar, what would you be?"

5. **Scripture Reading:** *selected by leader, group reflects*

6. **Accountability check:** *participants are invited to provide an update on quarterly SMART goals. These goals can be anything related to personal growth -- spiritual (such as reading a Bible passage); physical (walking); or relational (encourage at least one person three times each week.) The group helps each person select goals that fit their individual growth needs*

7. **Whole Health Action Management (WHAM):** *leader selects, and participants reflect on a topic to educate ourselves about faith and mental illness.* (i.e. How does forgiveness impact our mental health?)

8. **A Moment of Gratitude:** *participants are invited to lift up silent thanks for blessings received*

9. **Sharing:** *a time to talk about what is in your heart. We try to stay focused on current issues, not digging far into a person's past. In order to ensure all have an opportunity to share, the co-leader allots time and keeps things flowing.*

Our guidelines and agenda have been adapted slightly over the years we've been meeting, but not much. They are standing the test of time, which I believe indicates they have been Spirit-led. Individuals and groups throughout the country are now contacting me to find out more about our ministry. I share with them some of the tricks of the trade I have learned.

Meet once a week, every week. Like worship or AA, people need a place to come for spiritual encouragement on a regular basis. It is too hard to remember whether a group meets in varying weeks. For five years, we have met every Tuesday from 7:00-8:30 pm. This consistency allows people who may wander away from the group for a season to return and know we will be there.

Keep the focus on mental health struggles. While we have a loose definition of what qualifies a person to be a participant in the group, it is an understanding that we are there to receive spiritual encouragement for our wounded souls. We have no other business but to support one another and receive divine support.

Don't give advice. When someone interrupts another to tell them what to do, it can be demoralizing, both for the person sharing and for the group as a whole. Leaders have needed to be hyper-attentive to this as well as model this in our own speech.

The faithful friendships I have found in this group have been indispensable for my healing. I don't know what the future holds, but I trust that wherever we go, God will go with us. If not, we'd be better off disbanding and finding support elsewhere. Without the Spirit of the LORD guiding us, we will never experience what contributes toward our well-being. With the Spirit moving freely within and among the two or three or ten or more gathered, we can find healing for our souls.

~❖~

Don't let me ever think, dear God, that I was anything but the instrument for Your story-just like the typewriter was mine.

Flannery O'Connor

*May these words of my mouth and this meditation of my
heart be pleasing in your sight,
Lord, my Rock and my Redeemer.*

Psalm 19.14

CHAPTER THIRTY-TWO

blogging to build bridges

As early as the Winter of 2014, people were asking me when I would write another book. My speaking engagements were tapering off and momentum for *Delight in Disorder* was waning. Book sales were miniscule, which discouraged me. Now and then a reader would contact me with a moving testimony of how my book had touched them, but I knew that if I was going to reach more with the Good News for those impacted by mental illness, I needed to have another venue.

At that time I had a blog entitled *A Way With Words* where I explored a wide range of writing: devotions, spiritual essays, reviews, short stories, poems, etc… It was all over the map and while I had a number of followers, I was not engaging them much on the subject of faith and mental illness. I began to sense I was drawing more attention to myself than to Christ.

I was convinced that my writing was good enough to break into the secular arena, but countless rejections left me questioning this. My poems flash fiction, and short stories barely got a reading. On the other hand, my writing on spiritual topics was being readily accepted.

Songwriter John Prine writes in his song "Quiet Man," *Steady losing means you ain't using what you really think is right.* It seemed God was chipping away from me what I was not and leaving behind a more precise image of who I am, a person of faith living with a mental illness. So I left behind all my efforts to become known as the next J.D. Sallinger and focused on becoming the new Tony Roberts, one with a troubled mind who delights in the One who delights in me.

In the Spring of 2017, I created a new website, piggy-backing on the name of my book, *Delight in Disorder.* Thanks to the web design and coaching of Sean Pritzkau, I quickly developed a body of engaged readers who were exploring faith from the perspective of one impacted by mental illness.

I published two posts each week, which contributed to a consistent connection with followers and visitors. Soon, I began to receive emails from all over the U.S. and beyond, such as this one from Ian in the U.K.

My blog cultivated a mental health ministry in ways my book couldn't. My work is reaching laborers, advocates, seminary presidents, persons with mental illness, loved ones, and many more. Through personal stories and spiritual devotions, I foster friendship and cultivate compassion for those, like me, with troubled minds. Numbers have steadily increased, but even if I were the only reader, it would be worthwhile. I delight in writing, delight more when people read what I write, and even more when people respond to what I write. I am bolstered with the belief that my work is making a difference.

Like a typewriter (or keyboard) in the hands of God, my words are accepted by those seeking faith -- persons impacted by mental illness. Many are angry at God, Christians, and the Church. Some believe they are not worthy of God's love. Others feel like the Church has unfairly shunned them, that Christians are hypocrites who pick at the specks in the eyes of others while being blinded by the logs in their own eyes. My work aims to build bridges between two worlds that mean so much to me -- the world of the faith community, and the world of mental health. These worlds have been dangerously divided for years, at the expense of the lives of persons whose mindd betray them. Living in (but not of) both worlds, we cultivate compassion and foster friendships with those impacted by brain illnesses and gain insight into ourselves as wounded souls in need of God's grace to embrace our broken lives -- body, mind, and spirit.

*Embarking on this mission has required much soul-searching and devo-
tion on our part and we still wonder if we are up to the task. One thing
is clear, we are not. But with God's help and your prayers, Revealing
Voices will move from our heads into a world where faith and mental
illness have too long been divided at the
expense of wounded souls like us.*

Tony Roberts & Eric Riddle

*Praise be to the God and Father
of our Lord Jesus Christ, the Father
of compassion and the God of all comfort,
who comforts us in all our troubles, so we can comfort those in any
trouble with the comfort we ourselves receive from God.*

2 Corinthians 1.3-4

CHAPTER THIRTY-THREE

revealing voices

By the Fall of 2017, *Faithful Friends* and *Delight in Disorder* were on solid ground. Eric and I were both sensing a call to expand our outreach. Eric was listening to a wide variety of podcasts and had a dream to do one himself. But he knew he couldn't do one on his own. Perhaps God was knitting together his dream with our ministry for mental health.

We went for a walk one day, and he shared his idea with me. Not only had I never listened to a podcast, I was unfamiliar with the concept. Eric calmly walked me through the process of down-loading episodes, and I listened to some of his favorites, as well as others on the topics of faith and mental health. I quickly became convinced that not only was there a need for this ministry, but, with God's help, we could pull it off. Just as we did in the devel-opment of the *Faithful Friends* support group, we began to meet weekly to discover just what God had in mind.

We were both a little manic at the time. We had a grandiose notion that every word of the planning process was precious and needed to be recorded for future generations. Perhaps for a book on the modest beginnings of two world-renowned podcasters, rising from a basement study to a Manhattan studio. Maybe for a documentary, or feature length film. We were quite serious about our endeavor, but at the same time had a lot of fun.

Much of our early sessions dealt with parameters. Things like length of episodes, frequency, and format. We were ambitious, hoping to include a variety of segments such as interviews, essays, reviews, songs. Our first major creative difference was the length of episodes. Eric listened to many podcasts and was a fan of some that were as much as two hours or more. I didn't think we could hold the attention of listeners for more than 15 minutes. We settled on a 45-minute format, knowing that much editing would need to take place. We didn't know anything about the editing process yet, but Eric was confident we could learn as we went along. I, being a techno-newbie, had doubts.

Both Eric and I felt that if we were going to do this, we needed to do it well. We had listened to amateur podcasts that were sub-standard, both in terms of substantive content and production quality. We wanted to sound professional, and we knew we needed good equipment to pull it off. Neither of us had the resources to cover the cost, so, taking a page out of my *Delight in Disorder* publishing process, we conducted an Indiegogo crowd-funding campaign. With gifts ranging from $5 to $250, we met our goal and now had what we needed to produce a podcast that would speak to people who wanted more than two guys who sounded like they were in a tunnel, spouting off whatever was in their heads. We also used some of this patronage to fund a website, contract with a photographer, and recruit a sound engineer who recorded our theme music. We were thrilled with the results and headed into our first season eager to see what God would do.

We described ourselves as a mental health podcast that raised unanswered questions and shared unanswered prayers." We were "faith-based, peer-led, story-driven stigma-breaking." And, our signature question of each guest was, "What does healing mean to you?" We did not intend to be so much informational, not an advice program, but revelational, encouraging listeners to connect with both persons from a variety of perspectives, from professionals, to those personally impacted by mental illness.

We kicked off the season by interviewing Eric's wife, Jen, and my sister, April. They revealed their voices as caregivers, and, in our dialogue, Eric and I revealed who we were and how we lived with our illness.

The second episode we had Amy Simpson, author of *Troubled Minds: Mental Illness and the Church's Mission*. Amy revealed her voice as the child of a mother with a mental illness. She also shared the voices of persons throughout the faith community she had met who had the desire to do mental health ministry but lacked the tools and understanding.

Over the next two seasons, we interviewed pastors, politicians, parents, practitioners, and many others. It's hard to measure the impact numerically, but several folks have reached out to us personally with testimonies of how they were touched by the show.

Revealing Voices is still in its nascent stage. In the coming months and years, we hope to continue to reveal the voices of persons impacted by mental illness and use marketing and other techniques to reach more. I know we can't do this alone, but with the help of God working through the steadfast support of listeners and contributors, God only knows what can be done.

A Christian fellowship lives and exists by the intercession of its members for one another, or it collapses. I can no longer condemn or hate a brother for whom I pray, no matter how much trouble he causes me.

Dietrich Bonhoeffer

*There are different kinds of gifts,
but the same Spirit distributes them.
There are different kinds of service, but the same Lord. There are different kinds of working, but in all of them and in everyone it
is the same God at work.*

1 Corinthians 12.4-6

CHAPTER THIRTY-FOUR

mental health ministry

As 2019 rolled around, I had been out of pastoral ministry for over a decade. I attended worship but struggled to put my gifts to good use within church. Perhaps I was trying so hard not to be a church pastor that I didn't become an active participant either. My mental health ministry existed apart from my involvement in the local church. I longed for the rootedness in a body of believers who could support and encourage me as well as challenge and hold me accountable. That's when God led me to Pastor Mark Teike.

Mark has served as pastor of St. Peter's Lutheran for over 26 years. He has also been involved in NAMI and has referred several persons to *Faithful Friends*. He was one of the first guests on *Revealing Voices* and often commented on what an impact *Delight in Disorder* made on him personally and pastorally.

Pastor Teike invited Eric and I to deliver a keynote address on mental health ministry at the Heartland Conference of pastors and ministry leaders. It was then that my desire to serve within a church grew legs and started to move forward. I approached

Mark about serving St. Peter's as a Faith & Mental Health Advocate. I proposed the following responsibilities for my role:

- To equip staff to provide Christian care for persons with mental health challenges.

- To walk alongside persons impacted by brain illnesses, including loved ones.

- To cultivate compassion within the faith community for all who struggle with mental health issues.

Given my own limitations, we agreed I would work an average of only 5-10 hours each week. As it was a mission initiative, I would be supervised by the Life/Works director, Jan Kiel. I would also work closely with Pastor Teike to respond to needs within and beyond the congregation.

In the first year of my mental health ministry at St. Peter's, I have been involved in a broad range of activities. I have coached persons impacted by mental illness through crisis. I have discussed both pastoral and personal issues with staff over coffee or lunch. I have written articles, conducted interviews, and led small groups of people who often carry the mistaken notion that mental illness is a choice, not a medical condition.

Recent studies show 25% of the population will struggle with mental health issues in any given year. I've invited people in worship services to look around their pews. In front. To the left. To the right. If those people are okay, it's probably you. What I have learned, however, is that every time I have a confidential conversation with anyone, they reveal some issues they struggle with, often a diagnosis or that of a loved one. A teacher battling anxiety, fearful she is doing more harm than good. A pastor riding the emotional roller coaster of bipolar disorder. An administrator caring for an aging parent who is lapsing into depression caused by dementia.

It never ceases to amaze me how people open up when I tell them I am a Faith & Mental Health Advocate. My eye doctor told me about a brother with a mental illness who refuses to take his medicine and has given up on God. A chaplain talked about his teenage daughter who died by suicide. A man living on the streets shared his frustration that he could not get consistent care for his brain illness. I can't fix these problems, but when people reveal their voices of concern, grief, and anger, I can cry out with them to the One who alone hears and responds in love.

At our best, the church is a sanctuary where we can be who God created us to be. We can cultivate compassion as we follow the example of Jesus who reached out to those wounded — body, mind, and spirit. Jesus befriended those shunned by society and isolated from community.

The best way I know for a faith community to cultivate compassion and foster friendship with those who have mental illness is to come out of hiding and lead as wounded healers. At St. Peter's, I can be who I am and encourage others to be who they are created to be. Together in the Spirit of Christ, we can become an authentic community of faith where people with broken brains and hurting hearts find healing.

CHAPTER THIRTY-FIVE

focus on writing

Where do I go from here?

When I interviewed for the St. Peter's position, Mike Hinckfoot, Executive Director of Ministries, asked me, *This all looks great, but what will you give up to take this on?*

Everyone has limits. This is particularly true for someone like me who has an illness that can sometimes be debilitating. What can I do in ministry without burning myself out or burning someone depending on me?

My first strategy is to focus on time-flexible projects. Similar to when I was a student with essays or as I did in pastoral ministry with sermons, I get ahead when I am manic so as not to fall behind when I'm depressed. I also now have a body of work, over 500 sermons, and 1000 blog posts as well as countless devotions and journals I can recycle, reuse, or repurpose. It requires less time and energy to adapt than to create from nothing. Unless you're God, and I have learned the hard way, I'm not.

An aspect of my ministry God seems to be putting on my plate more and more is to encourage loved ones of those with mental illness. I am building relationships within groups such as the National Shattering Silence Coalition. Jeanne Gore and her cohorts are doing some incredible work there redefining what had been viewed as behavior problems into the brain illnesses they truly are.

In the coming months and years, I want to expand opportunities to reach loved ones with the compassion of Christ. Many have lost faith in a God who they believe has cruelly ignored tremendous suffering. Many find faith as a primary cause for psychological problems, as they have seen the damage of religious delusions. Still others have been stung by a shunning of faith communities, a place that should offer encouragement and support.

One step I am taking to reach loved ones is through my Facebook community *Hope for Troubled Minds.* Here we share concerns, inspirational quotes, advocacy opportunities, and other posts designed to build relationships that are supportive and uplifting.

Another step that is in the works will, Lord willing, become my third book. The working title is Hope for *Troubled Minds: God's Love for Those Who Love Persons with Brain Illnesses.* My plan is to interview many loved ones about their spiritual journey, their experiences in and out of the church, and how faith communities could best respond to the needs of those with troubled minds.

I'm praying those who read these stories will be inspired to cultivate compassion and foster friendship with those impacted by mental illness for the glory of God and the good of God's people.

I'm convinced the best way to break out of the prison of misery caused by mental illness is through building faith relationships. People with bipolar or other mental illnesses don't need an overabundance of mental health professionals, but we do need plenty of faithful friends.

Tony Roberts

*I no longer call you servants, because a servant does not know his master's business. Instead, I have called you friends, for
everything that I learned from my Father I have made known to you.
John 15.15*

~❖~

DIVERTED BY A PANDEMIC

If you want to make God laugh, tell him about your plans.

Woody Allen

Therefore, since we have been justified through faith, we have peace with God through our Lord Jesus Christ,
through whom we have gained access by faith into this grace in which we now stand. And we boast in the
hope of the glory of God. Not only so, but we also glory in our sufferings, because we know that suffering produces perseverance; perseverance, character; and character, hope. And hope does not put us to shame, because God's love has been poured out into our hearts through the Holy Spirit, who has been given to us.

Romans 5.1-5

CHAPTER THIRTY-SIX

assurance in anxiety

In late February of 2020, I was gearing up for another project at St. Peter's. I'd just finished leading a class called, *Walking Alongside Persons with Mental Health Challenges*. The counseling staff was calling on me more to encourage and support those impacted by mental illness, particularly loved ones. I had presented plans to produce a series of Q&A videos on Mental Health Ministry.

I finished the original draft of this manuscript and sent it off to Amy Simpson from Moody Publishing. She said it was good, but Moody was not looking for a memoir. She encouraged me to consider something more akin to a guidebook for loved ones. It seemed all signs were pointing in the direction of shifting my ministry from telling my own story of living with a mental illness to advising others how to best care for people like me.

Then came the end of the world, as we know it.

The COVID-19 crisis struck suddenly for many. In Indiana, we were given just two days notice that regular Sunday worship would be called off.

I led a staff devotion the day after the cancellation on Philippians 4.6 - *Do not be anxious about anything, but in every situation, by prayer and petition, with thanksgiving, present your requests to God.* I said this was not a stern command from a lawmaker intent on exposing our weaknesses, but a loving assurance from a Heavenly Father. Someone pointed out the verses within the full context of the letter..

Rejoice in the Lord always. I will say it again: Rejoice! Let your gentleness be evident to all. The Lord is near. Do not be anxious about anything, but in every situation, by prayer and petition, with thanksgiving, present your requests to God. And the peace of God, which transcends all understanding, will guard your hearts and your minds in Christ Jesus. (Philippians 4.4-7)

God is the peacemaker who quiets our hearts and minds during trials, not by demanding we be inhumanly stoic but by embracing us while we quiver with fear.

I had no idea during that Monday morning devotion just how much fear would strike so many.

Everybody knows that pestilences have a way of recurring in the world; yet somehow, we find it hard to believe in ones that crash down on our heads from a blue sky. There have been as many plagues as wars in history; yet always plagues and wars take people equally by surprise.

Albert Camus

Brothers and sisters, we do not want you to be uninformed about those who sleep in death, so that you do not grieve like the rest of mankind, who have no hope. For we believe that Jesus died and rose again, and so we believe that God will bring with Jesus those who have fallen asleep in him.

1 Thessalonians 4.13-14

~❖~

CHAPTER THIRTY-SEVEN

crashing and coming to

After I finished my devotion, Pastor Teike got up and offered more concrete words of assurance tempered with a large dose of uncertainty. Ministry would still go on, though only essential groups would meet. Someone asked about a recovery group. We don't know yet. When will we worship again? We don't know yet. We're waiting for word from the authorities. What will we do instead? We're still working on it.

What did we know? Very little.

The first thing Pastor Teike set forth for the staff was to arrange personal contacts to all members over 70, to determine their needs and meet them. If we could not meet as a church, then we would bring the church to them. I was so exhilarated about the challenge that I offered to contact five households by myself.

Then I came home and crashed.

A psychiatrist I once had said the nice thing about having rapid cycling bipolar is that if you don't like the mood state you're in -- hang on. It will pass quickly. The flip side of this is that if you are doing well, watch out. The floor will just as quickly fall in and you'll be left under a pile of rubble in the basement. These states shift with no advance warning and are often unrelated to external events. The pandemic that sent me into overdrive was now overwhelming me. I took to my bed where I stayed for most of March.

People who have occasional or even situational depression find it difficult to comprehend just how clinical depression could send someone into a near coma. I don't have a psychological answer, but I can testify personally that when I am at my lowest, I am so weighed down by guilt and shame I feel that if I got out of bed, I would do the world irreparable damage.

Instead, I lay there filled with regret. Dreadful visions of my past mingle with distorted voices in the present to riddle me with fear of the future. And not some distant future, but even the prospect of taking my next breath.

People also ask me how I could have served in pastoral ministry in such a condition. I say by the grace of God and with a lot of medication. Said better, it was God working through the pills and the prayers that kept me stable enough (often just enough) to be a faithful and sometimes fruitful pastor. With my disorder, I was like a trapeze artist with no sense of balance and when the winds of turmoil blew, I fell. In the midst of the pandemic, I was struck personally by a sudden blast.

My father has forever been my rock. He is the first to admit his failings, but even in doing so, his humility has laid a foundation for me. His self-deprecating humor, sharp wit, and generous spirit have won him many friends. To paraphrase what he says about others he admires, if you've got a problem with Dad, there must be a problem with you.

Dad has sucked the marrow out of life through hard living -- mostly chain smoking and consuming massive quantities of alcohol. It caught up to him around the time he turned 50. He quit cold turkey, but the damage had been done. The choices he made had taken their toll. In 2011, he had a major stroke that impaired his functioning, but not his spirit. Two years later he had open heart surgery and they told us he might not make it off the table. Since then he has had numerous risky surgeries and procedures that have forced us to face the prospect of Dad's mortality. In March of 2020, we discovered he has terminal cancer. The doctor has given him only months to live.

It's now May as I write this. I saw Dad this morning and he said he never felt better in his life. He always says that. The best pie ever is the one he has on his plate. The best experience ever is the one he is having. His best friend is the one he is with. He will go to his grave appreciating the best in all things.

At first the news of my father's diagnosis sent me deeper into depression. But I didn't get stuck there, thank God. God gave me the motivation to get out of bed and enjoy each moment I had with Dad. I believe Dad's faith and hope is rubbing off on me. I still get dismally depressed due to my diagnosis, but my perspective on it is improving. I don't let it get me down for any length of time. I don't heap guilt on shame and spend weeks in bed. Instead, I enjoy the best life has to offer, as Dad has taught me.

I believe Dad has peace with Christ and that he looks forward to a better life ahead. While the prospect of dying is not appealing, Dad maintains a sense of perspective. His humor remains intact. He once said that when they lay him in the ground, he would like a headstone pointed toward the road with a smiley face on it and the message, "I'm dead, but have a great day."

It won't be a great day when Dad dies, but it will be a day to celebrate the life of a great man.

The world is indeed full of peril, and in it there are many dark places;
but still there is much that is fear, and though in all lands love is now
mingled with grief, it grows perhaps the greater.

J.R.R. Tolkien

Rejoice with those who rejoice;
mourn with those who mourn.

Romans 15.12

CHAPTER THIRTY-EIGHT

hope for troubled minds

I was not the only one facing the prospect of a loved one dying. The COVID-19 crisis put all on alert that something could strike and take our breath away. Obituaries were filled with columns of names and messages that no gathering would be held. Closure was difficult to find and human touch to ease the depth of sorrow not allowed.

Once I came out of my own dark pit, I looked around and felt a tremendous sense of gratitude for God's many blessings in my life. Perhaps the greatest of these is the loving companionship of my wife, Susan. Our whirlwind romance has quickly become a bedrock for both of us.

The pandemic gives us the freedom to work together in our shared study at home with our loyal lab, Briley, at our feet. Susan has a passion for special education, particularly in correctional settings. We often discuss how our vocations overlap with so many persons who have mental illness in prison. Susan inspires me with her passionate care for the least of these, and when I feel I am one of the least, she inspires me all the more.

From a sense of gratitude, I reached out to others whose struggles I share. I started a Facebook group called *Hope for Troubled Minds*. Mania drove me to recruit members night and day and soon over 200 persons were part of our group, many of them actively participating. Loved ones of persons with a brain illness are most represented, followed by those with a diagnosis themselves. When the pandemic became a pressing mental health concern, I opened it up to all whose minds were troubled.

While not explicitly religious, our community raises deep spiritual issues. Persons from a broad range of background who have diverse perspectives converse about matters of the heart. The only rule I have established for our group is that we all *speak the truth in love,* and I have rarely had to enforce this. Community members respect each other, offering support through encouraging words, inspiring images, and uplifting songs.

Some of my evangelical brothers and sisters criticize me for being too "inclusive". I think we can be both evangelical and inclusive; in fact, I think it's essential, particularly in mental health ministry. Many of my brothers and sisters with brain illnesses have either turned away or been turned away from organized religion.

There's a dangerous divide between faith communities and those impacted by brain illness. Persons within the faith community feel the need to hide their diagnosis or a loved one's out of fear they'll be shunned. The only way to share the life-giving Good News with someone who has been filled with bad news is to show them the radical hospitality Christ showed in his ministry.

During pastoral ministry, I'd little interaction outside my church. My services were in such demand within the faith family that I formed few relationships outside of it.. Now I have the privilege of leading a community of diverse individuals seeking hope for their troubled minds. I share openly the hope I have in a loving relationship with Jesus Christ. I do so not to spark debate, but to invite dialogue that will show the way, reveal the truth, and invigorate life.

The function of prayer is not to influence God, but rather to change the nature of the one who prays...

Soren Kierkegaard

Therefore, confess your sins to each other and pray for each other so that you may be healed. The prayer of a righteous person is powerful and effective.

James 5.16

CHAPTER THIRTY-NINE

effective prayer

One way we deepen spiritual relationships within our community is through prayer. Some have been in pits of despair where our only prayers have been sighs too deep for words. We need the Spirit to pray for us and through us before we can intentionally express our own prayers.

Many with troubled minds distrust Christians who say, "I will pray for you," as a way to close the conversation or even cast judgement. Prayer should not be used as a club to beat someone over the head. As one of my professors once described prayer, it is a "long, loving look at the One who created us and wants what is best for us."

In *Hope for Troubled Minds*, I engage in a spiritual discipline of intercessory prayer where I message members, "How can I best pray for you?" My initial invitations went out to all 456 members at the time and I received over 300 responses. Sometimes it can feel overwhelming, but the thing about lifting up the longings of our hearts to the Lord is that our strength is increased, not depleted. I count it a privilege that people entrust me to join them in sharing their joys and burdens with the One who hears and responds in love. Even non-Christians are responding about the impact prayer makes, such as this exchange I had with my good friend I'll call Desiree --

Me: Hey Desiree, I'm devoting time this week to pray for our community members. How can I best pray for you?

Desiree: What a strange feeling I have as I ponder the question. I feel that your desire to pray for me, your wish to know HOW to pray for me…is about as good as any prayer. I simply can't tell you how to pray for me, because to do so would feel like I was accepting that there were ears to hear the prayer, a mind to process my need, and a divine will to act, or not. I hope you know my feelings and hopefully my "tone" is always coming from a place of love… Please don't feel like my comments about the prayer you would so graciously offer up for me are at all a "rejection." That you offer is a beautiful and loving act of kindness and friendship. I just come from a place of total unbelief.

Me: Yeah, I get that. Thank you for your gracious expression, friend.

About a week later, I wrote back to let people know I had been praying for them and ask how they were. I decided it would be fun to write to Desiree, so I did:

Me: As you requested, I have not prayed for you this week. Is there anything else you would like me to not pray for?

Desiree: This totally cracked me up! Mind if I share it, with your name cut out, of course? It would be in a positive way.

Me: You are welcome to share and include my name if you wish. It also cracked me up just thinking of it.

This was her post:

This message literally made me laugh out loud! My sweet friend Tony asked last week if he could pray for me. I told him the fact that he asked "HOW" he could pray for me was as meaningful to me as any prayer…but I couldn't begin to direct him how to pray for me or what to pray for. To do so would feel insincere, because I can't/don't believe there are ears to hear a prayer for me, or a divine will to act on it. (Been having a rough time emotionally due to the fact that I was impulsive and did something that hurt someone I love very much, blah blah blah…)

I then asked Desiree if I could share this exchange in a blog post and sent her a draft. She loved it and asked if she could share it on her Facebook page.

This is what she wrote:

My friend Tony is a beautiful human being. He's a Christian. I used to be a Christian. Now I'm an atheist. Once, this might have meant we couldn't find common ground. But being human is more than subscribing to a worldview. It's understanding that people who don't subscribe to yours are still worthy of grace and friendship and love. And yeah, it goes both ways.

Sometimes the best prayers are no prayers at all.

DUPLICATING THE PROCESS

So if you're walking down the street sometime
and spot some hollow, ancient eyes;
please don't just pass them by and stare
as if you didn't care.
Say hello in there.
"Hello."

John Prine

Ask and it will be given to you; seek and you will find; knock and the door will be opened unto you. For everyone who asks receives; the one who seeks finds; and to the one who knocks, the door will be open.

Matthew 7.7-8

CHAPTER FORTY

our common call

People with mental illness struggle with unresolved problems. This is a condition common to all human beings. We prefer to view life as a puzzle to figure out than a mystery to behold. Questions bother us. We want answers.

There are no clear answers when it comes to brain illness. While we are discovering more each day about the make-up and functioning of the brain, the amount we don't know is staggering. In the coming years, science hopes to explore this uncharted terrain, but for now we must act with more questions than answers.

As a Good News community, churches operate with some core theological truths:

All persons are created in the image of God.

Each of us is afflicted with a broken nature.

In Jesus Christ, we are healed by God's amazing grace.

Whatever shape mental health ministry takes, it needs to be built on these foundational truths. As we examine what we are doing and explore what can be done, this is the Good News we must share. People with brain illness are not problems to be fixed.

We do not represent a flaw in faith. While brain illnesses are a spiritual issue, they are not evidence of demonic possession.

Brain illness does not conclusively reveal the commission of sin any more than a physical affliction does. Instead, persons with brain illnesses are created in the image of God, broken by the inherited condition of sin, and in need of Christ's mercy for abundant life just like everyone else.

With these core beliefs firmly in place, we can create a mental health ministry that cultivates compassion and fosters friendship with those impacted by brain illness. We become partners in Christ's kingdom work where healing happens, maybe not as we would have it, but sure and certain.

So where do we begin? How about with a story of Jesus? The parable of the Good Samaritan. The man lying in the ditch was robbed of his ability to function independently.

Two leaders of the faith community pass him by because they put religion over relationships. They have lost touch of their shared sense of neediness on the empowering mercy of God and God's people.

Not so for the Samaritan. He knows all too well what it feels like to lie in a ditch, a ditch not of his own making, but one imposed on him by being considered one of the least. Sub-human.

Unlike the religious leaders, he sees the man in the ditch and is moved to take generous action. Not only does he lift the man up, but he transports him to an inn, and provides what is necessary for the man to heal.

Jesus asked who the neighbor to the man was lying helpless in a ditch. The answer is both obvious and hard to swallow. The neighbor was not who you would expect. Not the smiling pastor or the singing deacon. No, these go out of their way to put distance between themselves and the man in need. The true neighbor was the one who acted neighborly, the Samaritan who put relationship over religion and, in doing so, was the truly righteous one.

How can we be better neighbors for those most impacted by brain illness? First, get to know them. This may be quite difficult, as they may not only be lying in a ditch but covered with the dirt of shameful stigma. Many persons who battle a brain illness opt to do so alone rather than risk rejection from those who either can't or refuse to understand. They must then carry this burden of silence and fail to find the support they need.

But when we have eyes to see, it is easier to detect mental health issues. Who has unexpectedly stopped coming to church? Who is experiencing a series of unconnected physical ailments? Who is pulling away from friends and family? Isolating oneself is a sure sign that something is wrong; often that something is they are bearing the secret shame of a brain illness or mental health struggle.

If you see someone exhibiting such behavior, reach out to them. Begin with a casual connection like a card, email, or text. Let them know you miss them and that you are praying for them. If they don't respond at first, don't get discouraged.

Don't assume you did something wrong. I have found both personally and pastorally that prayers and encouraging words always make a positive difference. Even when they are not acknowledged, they are appreciated. They can be the first step towards lifting someone out of a ditch of despair.

Once we see those impacted by brain illness and approach them with compassion and love, what more can be done? I have described in this book how I did it, but you may be wondering if my method can be duplicated in your ministry setting. Yes. And no.

Yes! With God's help, you can cultivate compassion and foster friendship in a mental health ministry. Seek God where God is found: In the hands of the homeless unable to make sense of the world around them. In the eyes of the lost, locked away in prisons and jails for no better reason than they are deemed unsafe for society. In the hearts of the hopeless confined to psych units or secluded in their rooms.

Yet, no. You won't develop a fruitful mental health ministry if you are trying to help the "less fortunate." God doesn't listen when we say, "There, but for Your grace, go I," so much as when we say, "Here, with Your grace, am I."

There is hope, even when your brain tells you there isn't.

John Green

But God will never forget the needy;
the hope of the afflicted will never perish.

Psalm 9.18

CHAPTER FORTY-ONE

five questions and a quest

I was diagnosed with bipolar in 1995. Since then, not a day has gone by that I haven't about what it means to be a man of faith with a brain illness. As a pastor, I reflected deeply on how to do mental health ministry.

Now, my vocation is to equip, advocate, and walk alongside those impacted by brain illnesses. I have more questions than answers, learn something new each day, in every situation, and my teachers are those whom I serve and who serve me.

Over the course of my career, I've heard many questions from people wanting to get involved in mental health ministry. Here I share some of the questions, along with responses gleaned from personal and pastoral experience.

1. *How do I begin to develop a mental health ministry?*

Pray. Pray. Pray. Alone, plus with other ministry leaders, and with your congregation. By naming your desire, you both measure the harvest and call for laborers in the field.

2. *We are a small church, what difference can we make?*

You don't need to develop large programs to do faithful and fruitful mental health ministry. Small churches are uniquely positioned to be effective. People with mental illness don't need professional programs so much as personal friendships.

3. *What about leadership?*

Anyone can contribute to fruitful mental health ministry, particularly as a prayer warrior. The Enemy will devise any strategy at his disposal to subvert it. Ideally, however, leadership of your ministry will have personal experience with mental illness.

Consider bringing on board someone who has a brain illness yet who is stable enough to serve. In the secular arena, these persons are called peer recovery specialists. Having someone on your ministry team who can speak from experience and listen to the experiences of others builds trust and contributes to healing transparency.

4. *When do I know if it's time to begin a small group?*

I advise you to move slowly yet steadfastly. I receive contacts from pastors and other ministry leaders who are ready to rush into the fray without having first prayed, assessed the need, or recruited leadership. Eric and I devoted nine months to these things before our first meeting of Faithful Friends. I believe this has contributed greatly to our effectiveness and longevity.

5. *What else can I do?*

Much. With the aim of bridging the dangerous divide between the faith community and persons impacted by brain illnesses, you want to avoid creating a separate program for mental health ministry. Instead, bring persons with mental health issues into the life and leadership of the whole ministry.

According to the gifts they have, include them as worship leaders, Christian educators, committee members, and in other roles. Ask them to share their testimony of how God has helped them in the midst of their struggles. Encourage them to name specifically their diagnosis and how God has strengthened them in the midst of their challenges.

These are just five questions to consider. You may have others. If you do, I would be delighted to respond. Please send them to me here: tony@delightindisorder.org.

There is a cacophony of voices out there criticising the Church in particular and believers in general for failing to accept persons with brain illnesses, for cultivating a climate of stigma that does what can sometimes be irreparable damage to a person's soul. I know this happens. I've witnessed it. But I've also experienced in my life and ministry something quite different. I know first-hand what is possible when we are open and honest about our struggles, when we take the risk of careful and prayerful disclosure, when we are guided by the Holy Spirit of acceptance rather than the demonic spirits of false judgement.

Once Jesus was wandering the hillside, perhaps taking a break from the demanding crowds (Matthew 5.1-20). He encounters a man with an "impure spirit" unable to be contained, cutting himself with stones. The man had been excluded, or excluded himself from society, and was living in tombs like a dead man.

When he saw Jesus, the man recognized a unique power about him. Jesus spoke directly to his affliction, calling on the unclean spirits to flee. Then, in an amazing and incredible way, Jesus commanded the spirits to leave the man and later we find him at peace, in his right mind, sharing his testimony of how Christ had healed him.

Though not indicative of demon possession, there are important parallels between this man's story and those of us who have a brain illness. First, there is exclusion. Second, there is self-harm. And third, there is healing in an encounter with Christ.

First, exclusion can be powerful, strong enough to rob us of any connection with community. Such exclusion is frequently laid upon us by persons who fail to understand our illness and who are afraid. Ignorance breeds contempt and contempt fuels exclusion. The stigma that flows from this is all too often internalized. We begin to believe the press clippings that our life is not worth living and that we would be better off dead.

This death-dealing message leads to self-harm. For some this takes an almost identical version as the man's -- cutting. For others, it is more subtle, but just as damaging. Drinking and other drugs. Reckless living. Not eating, sleeping, or engaging in activities that contribute to good health. In some cases, the pinnacle of self-harm -- suicide.

Yet, there is hope. The Spirit of Christ finds us among the living dead and addresses our needs directly. Jesus does not skirt the issue with this man. He doesn't talk around the subject of his affliction, choosing instead to discuss the weather, sports, or the economy. Jesus invites even the damaging aspects of ourselves to come out into the open. It is through this openness that his festering wounds can breathe in refreshing air and begin to heal.

Don't get me wrong. I have not been cured of my brain illness, and I don't expect to be in this life. But I can live with it, thanks to the healing mercy of Christ and the Holy Spirit flowing through the faith community. I believe this is possible for all my friends and family who struggle with troubled minds. Healing happens when we walk together out of the destructive darkness and into the healing light.

This is my story.

Now tell me yours.

~✧~

EPILOGUE

challenges and hopes

Studies show as many as 1 in 5 persons will experience symptoms of mental illness in a given year. This can be debilitating, leading to loss of jobs, relationships, even lives. If you experience depression, anxiety, obsession, see a doctor. There is hope, but we must first ask for help.

Some discover when seeking help we have a brain illness, like bipolar disorder, schizophrenia, and major depression, posing risk factors that threaten our stability and endanger our lives According to statistics the National Institute on Mental Health (NIMH) and the National Alliance on Mental Illness (NAMI):

- In couples with at least one partner who has a brain illness, divorce rates are as much as 80% higher.

- 35% receiving disability benefits have a mental health diagnosis.

- There are 1,000 visits a year to emergency departments due to mental health issues.

The initial prognosis I received was not an exaggeration. If anything, it shielded me from some of the even more harsh realities individuals with bipolar disorder face:

- Estimations show 82.9% of people living with bipolar have serious impairment.

- Bipolar life expectancy is 20 years below average.

- Over 15% of us take our own lives.

What hope can be found? Remember, *It doesn't have to be this way.* And, *It may not be this way much longer.*

Research is expanding treatment options in areas such as:

- Pharmacogenomics - genetic testing to select the best medication for patients.

- Deep brain stimulation - electrodes regulate neurological activity (like a pacemaker).

Brain illness is more of a mystery than a puzzle, but God is guiding science to develop new ways to dig deeper into the mystery so there is less suffering.

ACKNOWLEDGEMENTS

gratitudes

People ask if my books are self-published and I find this difficult to answer. *A Way With Words* is my own imprint and, as yet, I am the only author we have published. But *Delight in Disorder* and *When Despair Meets Delight* are far from solo projects. I am the Chief Shepherd of many other shepherds who each have vital responsibilities to care for the flock.

Some of the co-shepherds of this book include:

My mother **Patsy Kurtz**, who gave me birth and her husband **Dan**, who gave me a place to call home.

My father **Veston** and his wife **Connie**, who showed me how to be generous with your care.

My aunt **Rose Harper** and her husband **Richard** who helped me feed the lambs until they were ready to be weaned.

My wife **Susan**, who was patient with me when I stayed up all night tending the flock.

Beta readers **Jen Riddle, Kathy DiDomizio**, and **Katie Dale** who groomed the fleece.

I would be remiss if I didn't acknowledge the inspiration of the Holy Spirit, the God I have come to know in Jesus Christ. If there is anything in here that is good and kind and loving, it is from the divine spirit of Christ. The rest is my own disordered mind getting in the way.

~❖~

BIBLIOGRAPHY

works cited

All Biblical citations, unless otherwise noted, are from THE HOLY BIBLE, NEW INTERNATIONAL VERSION®, NIV® Copyright © 1973, 1978, 1984, 2011 by Biblica, Inc.® Used by permission.

Other translations used: The Holy Bible, King James Version (KJV), public domain.

New Revised Standard Version Bible (NRSV), copyright © 1989 the Division of Christian   Education of the National Council of the Churches of Christ in the United States of America. Used by permission.

Allen, Woody. *Without Feathers.* New York: Random House, 1975

Becker, Ernest. *The Denial of Death.* New York: Simon & Schuster, 1973

Bernanos, Georges.. *The Diary of a Country Priest.* Public domain, 1936

Bonhoeffer, Dietrich. *Life Together: The Classic Exploration of Christian Community,* New York: Harper One, an imprint of Harper Collins Publishers, 1954 [2009]

Buechner, Frederick. *Wishful Thinking: A Theological ABC.* New York: Harper & Row, 1973

Camus, Albert. *The Plague.* US: Hamish Hamilton, 1948

Chambers, Oswald. *My Utmost for His Highest.* Public domain, 1935

Chandler, Raymond. *The Long Goodbye.* US: Houghton Mifflin, 1953

Chesterton, G.K. *Orthodoxy.* Garden City, N.Y.: Image Books, 1959

Coelho, Paulo, and Margaret Jull Costa.. *The Zahir*: a novel of obsession. New York: HarperCollins, 2005

Cowper, William, *God Moves in Mysterious Ways from Olney Hymns and other Sacred Works.* Public domain, 1779

Frost, Robert. *Death of a Hired Man,* 1915

Green, John. *Turtles All the Way Down.* New York: Dutton Books, 2017

Greene-McCreight, Kathryn. *Darkness Is My Only Companion.* Grand Rapids, MI: Brazos Press, 2006

Hankey, Kathryn. *Tell Me the Old, Old Story* Public domain, 1866

Jamison, Kay Redfield. *An Unquiet Mind: A Memoir of Moods and Madness.* New York: Vintage Books, 1995

_____ . *Night Falls Fast: Understanding Suicide.* New York: Knopf Kempis, Thomas a. 1420-1427 *The Imitation of Christ.* Public domain, 1999

Latner, Joel. *The Gestalt Therapy Book: A Holistic Guide to the Theory, Principles, and Techniques of Gestalt Therapy Developed by Frederick J. Perls and Others.* Center for Gestalt Development, 1986

Lewis, C.S. *The Four Loves.* New York: Harcourt, Brace, Jovanovich, 1960

Mabbott, Thomas Ollive. *Edgar Poe and His Critics.* New York: Rudd & Carleton, 1860

Manning, Branning. *The Ragamuffin Gospel: Good News for the Bedraggled, Beat-Up,and Burnt Out.* Colorado Springs: Multnomah Books, 1990

Nouwen, Henri J.M. *The Wounded Healer as a Spiritual Guide.* Image Books, 1979

_____ . *Life of the Beloved: Spiritual Living in a Secular World.* New York: Crossroad, 1992

Obama, Barak. *The Audacity of Hope: Thoughts on Reclaiming the American Dream.* New York: Crown Publishers, 2006

O'Connor, Flannery. *The Complete Stories.* New York: Farrar, Straus and Giroux, 1971

Peter, Laurence J. *The Peter Principle.* New York: William Morrow & Co. Inc., 1969

Plath, Sylvia. *The Unabridged Journals of Sylvia Plath,* 1950-1962. New York: Anchor Books, 2000

Prine, John "Hello in There" *Beyond Words* Nashville, TN: Oh Boy Records, 2017

Roberts, Tony. *Delight in Disorder: Ministry, Madness, Mission,* Columbus, IN: A Way With Words Publishing, 2014

Solomon, Andrew. *The Noonday Demon: An Atlas of Depression.* New York: Scribner, 2001

Steinbeck, John. *Travels with Charlie: In Search of America* New York: Viking Press, 1962

Stevenson, Robert Louis. *Lay Morals* Public domain, 1911

Szasz, Thomas Steven. *Cruel Compassion: Psychiatric Control of Society's Unwanted* Syracuse, NY: Syracuse University Press, 1994

Tolkien, J.R.R. *The Fellowship of the Ring.* UK: Allen & Unwin, 1954

ABOUT THE AUTHOR

Tony Roberts is a man with a troubled mind who delights in the One who delights in him. He enjoys going out to dinner with his wife Susan, talking with his children on FaceTime and spontaneous adventures. If he were a candy bar he would likely be Almond Joy. Connect with him on the *When Despair Meets Delight* facebook page.

a
Way With Words
publishing
Columbus, Indiana
USA

A Way With Words publishing, based in Columbus, Indiana, is the imprint for *Delight in Disorder Ministries* and produces work

sharing hope for troubled minds.

Join the Facebook group *Hope for Troubled Minds.*

The group provides spiritual support for those battling mental illness and those who love them.

We journey together, fostering hope with encouraging words, uplifting songs, and inspiring images.

We listen with care, speak the truth in love, and in doing so promote the best healing together.